THE VICTORY OF SURRENDER

THE VICTORY OF SURRENDER

by

Otis Carney

Cover Photography by John Fandek

By the same author:

LOVE AT FIRST FLIGHT (with Charles Spalding)
WHEN THE BOUGH BREAKS
YESTERDAY'S HERO
GOOD FRIDAY 1963
THE PAPER BULLET
NEW LEASE ON LIFE
WELCOME BACK, BILLY RAWLS
CHIHUAHUA 1916
THE FENCE JUMPER
EDDIE BULWER'S GROUND
THROW THE RASCALS OUT
FRONTIERS
ISLAND GIRL
HOG HEAVEN

To David for the change
To Teddy for the life

"Behind the night---somewhere afar
some white tremendous daybreak."
　　Rupert Brooke

"Toto, I've a feeling we're not in Kansas anymore."
　　Dorothy
　　<u>Wizard of Oz</u>

You've probably never thought of yourself as being in a war.

I certainly didn't. Long ago I paid my dues in one and when we'd finally blown it away, I figured it was all over Over There. Thank God.

If you're male, you've been raised on war. It's expected of you. Men fight, men win, whether you like it or not. If you're female, the idea of war repluses you even more. It means killing life. You're the bearer of life. You protect it instinctively, which is why you'd never dream of being in a war let alone being told that you'd better give it up if you want victory in your life.

The war you and I live in doesn't have any winners. It makes a few heroes, we think, but sooner or later they all troop off into the darkness. The war that you and I fight every day is in the battleground of your head, your emotions, your consciousness.

The walking wounded are the ones who didn't learn early enough how not to fight it. The killed in action are the ones who never stopped trying to beat it and win.

The war is in your business, your supermarket, your TV. It's in traffic, commuting, the price you pay for gasoline. It's in your voting, your kids soccer games, in the words you use, the thoughts you hold. It's in your body language, the look on your face. It's in your bank account and your marriage bed. It's even out on a slope skiing, or in a stream with a trout.

The war is your survival. It is being waged right now, this moment, in how you are being forced to live in the last hours of the most warlike of all centuries, the 20th.

You can go down fighting in defeat and die. Or, you can stop fighting, surrender and live.

One thing is certain. The war won't go away. It can't. It's too deep in your heart for you to seek a separate peace.

The only way to declare an armistice is in your head. Time to stack the rifles and let the bugles blow no more.

You already know where true peace is. You just don't know you know it---yet.

If you go looking for it, you won't find it.

If you let go and let it find you, it will.

1.

There are two islands out there. One is dark, a hell hole. The other is light, a paradise. If you're like me, you seem to spend your life running back and forth between the two, waiting for that happy day when you'll finally learn how to quit and get off the world for good.

The second island isn't something dreamed up by a travel agent. Paradise is its actual name. It's so far out in the western Pacific that you know you're off the world when you reach it. The first island, Pelelieu, though equally distant, is a place you wouldn't want to be caught dead on---and just might.

From the air it looks like a lobster claw, cut off from its body and left to rot in a green, fetid sea. Its open pincers are trapping a blood-red mangrove swamp, and the shell of its claw is a shattered white spine of coral. Umurbrogol, the Palauan natives call it. The Marines had another name. Bloody Nose Ridge---"that stinking sonofabitch."

On Pelelieu's corpse of flotsam, three miles wide by five miles long, in a firestorm lasting forty days and forty nights, 22,000 humans would be wounded or killed. Eleven thousand of them were Japanese, all but 35 dead. Five thousand of ours never came back to their Gold Star mothers. The rest of us limped on home, still wondering why. What had it all been for?

In my own small way, I must have been trying to answer that question. On the morning of October 14, 1944, I was a Marine Corps first lieutenant, sitting under the belly of my plane on the Pelelieu runway. I was typing a novel about love and war. Light and dark. I'd lifted the title from the Bible: "One Will be Taken, One Will be Left." In short, which one? Hopefully not me.

When you're 22 years old, still cocky enough to be in love with the adventure of war, you pretty much learn to insulate yourself from any downside. After all, we could have been riflemen up on the ghastly Ridge, instead of having a plane to soar away on and escape the heat for a moment or two.

Though no fault of mine, I'd lucked into good duty. I was flying for a grand, rugged general, Roy Geiger, who commanded half the Marines in the Pacific. Our main job was to get him in and out of the islands where his people were fighting, and to keep ourselves from getting shot in the meantime. If and when we ever managed to sneak off to Hawaii, the Old Man made sure we'd have a precious jeep of our own and a curfew pass. While thousands of lonely lovers were mourning in their blacked-out barracks, we'd be carousing all over Oahu. Our only deadline was when the general blew his whistle, and we'd have to go join him on some steaming rock where nobody danced or wore pikaki leis.

Also, that morning on Pelelieu, I'd fashioned myself as a budding author. Through another lucky break, while we were in flight training, an old friend and I had written a novel. We pooled our experiences as cadets, and he put down most of the words. My main contribution was to stumble onto the title, <u>Love at First Flight.</u> To our amazement, people bought it, but they more or less had to, being a captive audience. Right then, thousands of other kids were learning to fly. After Mom's cookies and the knitted hats had run out, what better to send the family cadet than a few pages of laughs before he had to roar off into the wild blue yonder? Though the book was clinging to the best-seller lists, by now I was determined to paste one up there all by myself. Solo flight this time. Give 'em the real McCoy war.

I had a box seat for it on Pelelieu. A half mile from me, Geiger's marching Marines were hurling themselves against Bloody Nose Ridge. It was a fortress the Japanese had been building for years, a rat warren of caves and interlocking fields of fire. We'd shelled it, napalmed it, turned it into a stinking smoking moonscape of naked coral. A thousand Marines had already been lost trying to scale one slope of the Ridge no bigger than a football field. As I tried to type what I hoped was my epic novel, the clicking keys of my battered old Hermes portable made a sound very much like the sniper bullets which, at random, would crack and hiss in our direction.

But the love part of the novel was harder to explain. Why,

2

right at that moment, was I groping to find a name for my heroine? Six years earlier, when I was sixteen, I'd written my first novel and it had plenty of love in it. After visting Gettysburg and Fort Sumter, I'd fallen in love with the South and the epic tragedy of the Civil War. My heroine had to be a southern girl. I'd known a few when I was a boy, hunting quail down in Mississippi. These were soft, languid young things who'd melt against you when you danced and whisper gently in your ear---everything I wanted in love, and a far cry indeed from the starchy Yankee girls in my Chicago dancing school. So I made my heroine into the willowy, magnolia-scented Gwendolyn Guerin, a brown-haired graceful patrician from a Low Country plantation.

But now, that morning at Peleliu, I was stuck for a heroine again. In my new novel, I was writing pure homesickness, trying to escape from the noise and obscenity of the war swirling around me. Longingly, I was revisiting my boyhood, the games and girls and dreams we'd had in the Chicago suburb of Lake Forest. But what girl? Who would she be? The exact right name is essential for a novelist. It colors everything you write about the lady.

Into my head popped "Teddy." I'd never known anybody with that name. Oh, maybe a boy when I was a kid, but not for a girl.

Yet it seemed to fit what I wanted. I typed Teddy several times, filled out her first scene and then put the page down at my feet. I had a couple of hundred pages written thus far. I was using flimsy Japanese rice paper we'd liberated out of a supply dump on Guam during the battle earlier in the summer. The pages were original only, no carbons. My typewriter was perched on two gas cans, and I kept my precious pages from blowing away by putting coral rocks on top of them.

But writing was not my only job at that moment. For some bizarre reason, considering that I can barely boil water, I'd appointed myself cook for our plane crew. While I'd been off on my flight of fancy with my new heroine, the radioman, crewchief and my partner pilot, Cecil Matney were hungry for breakfast. Our single meal whenever we could get it was basically dog food, meat and beans in a can. To be able to choke it down, we had to heat it, which we did by taking a metal cartridge box liner, punching holes in it, filling the bottom with sand, and soaking it with aviation gas from the sumps of our plane. But unfortunately, just now, our old stove had melted, so I said to our crewchief, "Over there, Mel. That ought to be an easy place to find us a new liner."

I was pointing at a Japanese coral revetment about a hundred feet from the plane. In the circular enclosure lay the blackened skeleton of a Betty bomber, plus about a ton of every kind of ammunition anybody could shoot. Aerial torpedoes, mortar and artillery shells, thousands of rounds of machine gun and rifle ammo. The attacking Marines had dumped it here on their way to the big fight against the Ridge.

Mel started out toward the revetment. About half-way there, he stopped and hollered at me: "Hey, Mr. Carney, this damn thing is smoking. You don't suppose it could go off?"

Well, everything was smoking on Pelelieu. Bullets were whistling everyplace anyway. "Oh, hell, no," I started to say, "it'll never…."

Varoom!

The world exploded. A roar, giant flash of flame, then sickening, popping, chattering ammo catching and blowing. The coral runway was throbbing, earthquaking in the blasts, our plane bouncing up and down on its tires, the undercarriage creaking. Half-naked Marines were shouting, running past us, some hit and bleeding, one man with a jagged sizzling fragment protruding from his shoulder.

We were on ground zero, chunks of metal hissing over us and some crashing down like deadly hail. In abject terror, I was running around beneath our plane like a marble in a teacup, eight hundred gallons of high octane gas inches above my head. Let one fragment stike---well, I wasn't thinking, couldn't think. Cece Matney was shouting, "Get the plane outa here!" Nobody ever had a better idea!

I followed him, racing up through the darkened cabin and hitting the start switches before we'd even sat down. Mel, the crewchief, had warmed the engines up earlier, so in the miracle of it they caught in the first go-around. Mat roared the throttles to the firewall. We jumped the chocks and went on a screaming taxi as far away as we could get from the inferno. And not far enough, considering Pelelieu's minimal land area, half of which was still being held by the enemy.

We lept out of the plane and took shelter in a coral ditch. By now, the whole dump was blowing, screaming rounds of every kind of shell roaring above us, random, unseen, inglorious stuff of our own making, to kill us with. For two hours we lay in that ditch, up to our bellies in stagnant rain water. For my part of it, I was shaking all over. I'd been shelled before on Bougainville and Guam, but nothing like this. These were mindless enemies, not caring who they blew up.

When it was over and the ambulances were carrying the wounded away, we taxiied back to our parking spot on the strip. My Hermes portable was a black crab squashed into the coral. And my two hundred plus pages of love and war? In the roaring run-up of our escape, our engines had blown them all over the island.

A few days later, a half-naked, bearded Marine came down from the Ridge. He had a few of my precious pages crumpled in his hand. Scuttlebutt was, he said shyly, some fly boy down here had been writing a book. The riflemen in his platoon had found some of it and had been using it as toilet paper---until they began reading the stuff and figured it might mean something to somebody.

I later re-wrote it from memory. If it was bad at first, it was dreadful done twice. But something more than a book was at work here.

Not quite two years after my love/war dream blew away, I was back finishing up at Princeton. I'd run off to flight training a couple of months after Pearl Harbor. We didn't want to miss a minute of it, and prayed the war wouldn't end before we'd had our shot at it.

But playing college boy again was an awful drag. After four years of having life or death in our hands, now to return and be treated like industrial school cadets was more than I could stomach. The Nassau Hall authorities wouldn't even let us cut a class to go up to New York and find a job. Further, it was June 21st. I had a long steamy summer ahead at Princeton, just to cram myself full of such vital knowledge as Chaucerian English and the Lake School of poets.

I was at the bottom of a pretty dismal barrel. I'd just ended a passionate affair with a girl who was wonderful but when she wrote me almost daily, I could feel the dreaded noose tightening. Wedding bells, the end of my freedom. Oh my God, that was terrible fly paper to try to get loose from. Earlier, I'd been able to lose myself in baseball and tennis, but now the seasons were over. With six eye-glazing courses on my back, I was so worn out that my only escape seemed to be coming down with one of those traditional, please-Daddy-help-me-colds. Late that afternoon, I'd worked myself up to fever and chills. I was lying in a fog of Vicks Vapo-rub, staring at the wall of my bedroom in the eating club where we lived.

Then in came my roommate. He was tying his tuxedo tie. "Get off your ass," he said. "Stop feeling sorry for yourself." We were going to a party, a debut up in nearby Far Hills. He'd already pulled the time-worn stunt of wiring the hostess and asking if he could bring his houseguest.

Reluctantly, I crawled into my own tux. Another crasher joined us en route. We hit the party as almost the first guests to arrive. When the hostess scowled at me, I took refuge in the bar and tried to get a drink. The waiters were sorry, sir, but only champagne was being served. I can't stand the stuff and finally worked a waiter into cadging me some Scotch from our host's private stock. With a few sips in me, the only place left to hide seemed to be the dance floor.

I turned and under the stately green and white marquee happened to see a girl. Actually, she was the first female guest to arrive. She had a loveliness about her that caught my attention. She was willowy, long brown hair, and wearing a flowing ball gown of white tulle. A smallish young man had brought her to the party. He seemed to be enjoying her immensely while they danced. Finally, I couldn't stand it.

I tapped him on the shoulder and cut in. I gave her my name. She gave me hers.

"Teddy."

OhmiGod! Teddy? Teddy what?

"Fly."

"You mean Fry?" I stammered.

She laughed gently. "No, Fly. F-L-Y. Teddy Fly. It's short for Frederika. We have names like that down South."

South? Teddy? Gwendolyn Guerin? She had to be, didn't she! I wasn't dancing, I was soaring. No, she wasn't from South Carolina, but Memphis, Tennessee. And a plantation? Well, actually, they used to have them down in Mississipi, but the only one left now in the family was a dreary place in Arkansas.

By then, I was lost in her. She was fascinated that I wanted to be a writer. We swapped lies about how much T.S. Eliot we had read. I faked it with the one line I could remember from The Love Song of J. Alfred Prufrock: "I grow old, I grow old, and I wear the bottoms of my trousers rolled." She wanted to be a writer too, she confessed, and someday longed to live out on the land. My dream exactly. I'd spent much of my youth out hunting birds in the cornfields of Illinois. Someday I'd get a farm of my own, even a ranch. Land-love, I craved it. As we danced on and on, I was so busy holding my fantasy in my arms that it finally dawned on me that we were hopelessly stuck with each other. This was her first debut party and she didn't know anybody here. She was only 18, three days after her graduation from boarding school in Virginia.

Finally, as good southern girls are taught, she didn't want to be a burden to me. She'd slip off to the ladies room and give me a chance to find someone else, if I wanted. *Who else,* for God's sake! I had it all in her, didn't I?

The ladies room was on the second floor of the old colonial house where the party was being held. With a little wave at me, my new Teddy went up the long staircase and I waited urgently at the bottom. By then, a few of my college friends had spotted me. Many of them were married by that time and were always ragging me because I couldn't seem to find my own real thing.

I just have, I crowed. This girl is really something, fresh out of school, a true southern beauty. "Look," I said, and pointed up at the top of the stairs.

There my discovery stood, all grace and poise. Smiling, knowing we were watching her, Teddy took the first dainty step, tripped, and came tumbling down the entire staircase in a flailing ball of tulle. After I got the poor thing picked up and brushed off, my old pals winked at me and drifted away. "Nice try, Ote." Quit robbing the cradle, will you? Get one with a little age on her, who at least knows how to walk.

What they didn't know, nor did I, a year from that very night, in Memphis, Tennessee, I'd be brushing the rice off her, and in the fifty-two years since, she's never made another false step.

Did she fall or was she pushed?

Who would ever have written such an outrageous plot?

Surely not me!

But yes, me. I was the maker of it. I'd dreamed it up myself in some strange way I didn't yet know I knew. It would be fifty years before I'd learn what it was. And learn the hard way that in my new war, the only victory I could seek now would have to be surrender.

2.

A half century later, on a beautiful morning in Wyoming, I seemed to have everything anybody could possibly want.

Teddy was with me. We had three wonderful sons, six grandchildren, good health and the blessing of being able to live out on land that we loved. Years before, we'd taken an old cattle ranch, sagging log buildings, sweat and tears of the pioneers, and had turned it into our dream. Our kids had grown up on it, and now theirs would come for visits that were always too short. I'd persuaded my brothers and sister to buy the adjoining ranch. In the summers, nieces, nephews and their children would be biking over for tea with Aunt Teddy. Together we'd be cowboying, hunting, fishing, and on picnic nights up in the timber, country western music on the kids' guitars.

Of course there were a few thorns in the rose. Cattle, roaming the sagebrush, and in our mountain paradise---furthest town in the U.S. from a railroad---forty below in the winters, fifteen feet of snow---probably the hardest place in America we could have picked to raise a cow. As a cattle buyer once said to me, feasting his eyes on our splendid isolation, "You've got game, you've got fish, got it all. Do you know what I'd do if I had this place?"

"What?"

"Sell it and get a cattle ranch. "

But then again, our neighbors would tell us, "Just hang on. Calf market's bound to get better one of these years. This is a business for stickers."

When my father first saw the ranch, he shook his head bleakly. "How did you ever find such a godforsaken place? What in hell will you do with it?"

DO? Could we do nothing? Just more or less BE? Be in life, be who we were, be in love, be in God.

"Not for profit," he snorted. "God help you."

He did. And in the years, we slowly came to know that we

weren't here for bottom lines.

That morning in August, I was out doing what I loved best, floating lazily down the Green River which flows through the meadows and willow bottoms just below our rock house.

We'd built on a high bluff overlooking the river because it gave us a see-forever view of the Wind River mountains to the east, and vast sweeps of sagebrush to the west. Part of the old Oregon trail crossed here, the wagon ruts still in the grass, and occassionally the glint of a button, an oxen shoe or a bullet dropped from a wagon. The site of the house was a circle of white rocks where the Shoshone Indians had had a sweat lodge. For centuries, they'd cooked themselves here in the smoke of sweet sage, and when they'd deemed themselves adequately purified, they'd take a deep breath and plunge into the icy water below.

When we'd taken our own plunge and built the house, there were a few minor details we'd ignored. Trees, for one, shrubs, anything to screen us. We were sitting up there naked as a sore thumb. In our high country, we'd dig up little aspen and pines and stick them into the sandy soil. Teddy would be out watering them late into the indian summer nights. Next morning or next week, in would howl old man winter, snow banking several feet up the windows. Rabbits, squirrels, moose, even mice would start going to work on our garden, rooting up the only green left in the country. "But Harry," Teddy pleaded to the beloved old Seabee who had built our house, "can't we get *anything* to grow?"

Harry scratched his bald head and took another pinch of snuff. "Teddy," he said, "I reckon if God wanted trees on this here bluff, he would have put 'em here."

So in the end, as a last stab at landscaping, I sawed and hammered up a buck fence around the house---probably my only carpentry since Manual Training class in 4th grade, and I was still flunking. My younger brother, Peter, looked at the house and shook his head. "Why don't you get a bugler and a flag, and you can call it Fort Carney?"

But our homesteading days seemed far behind us, that morning on the Green. Two old friends were with me in my tin john boat. They were to learning how to fly fish, which meant, in their anxious lashes, I'd get their line whipped around my neck, or one of their flies hung up in a willow on the bank. The Green has a powerful current. It supplies most of the water for the Colorado River. Though I'd done it for thirty seven years, rowing upstream against the current is tilting at an awfully big windmill. I'd dig the oars into the crystal water or slide us into the bank where I could grab branches and hand-over-hand us upstream. Sometimes I'd just say the hell with it and break off the fly. They had boxes of brand new ones from Orvis anyway, so we could let a few go for the birds to pick at.

But there was something else I mustn't have been letting go. After the morning's exertion and lunch, I lay down to take a nap. Sleep didn't come. I was twitchy. My heart felt strange and started missing beats. My neck began to hurt. Now what the devil is going on, I asked myself? I've always been healthy as a horse, forty years out on these ranches, hunting, fishing, trying to beat a dollar out of a cow. The poor man's fox hunt. As a friend of mine said, "Carney, with the exception of whoring, has it ever occurred to you that you've spent most of your life in the two oldest, lowest paid callings in the history of mankind: the telling of tales and the pasturing of beasts?"

Well, sure, because we love it, we want to do it. But what was different about today? I expect summers to be furious up at the ranch, not only our big family but plenty of friends with fly rods. Dry dudes, we call them, the non-paying kind, and they're a delight to share the place with. I do a lot of chasing around trying to find them fish. Then, too, it *is* a business, so we put the dudes to work, pick out our gentlest horses, saddle them up and pray that nobody gets dumped between here and there. We have cattle to move, riding long hours in the sagebrush hills, jogging behind the tails of beasts. If I have my own world by the tail, I kept asking myself, why is it that I still can't sleep or extinguish the trip-hammer thumping in my chest?

I toughed it out for a couple of days, and finally got a little scared. After a two hour drive to an emergency room, a doctor I'd never seen before told me what was wrong. Arrythmia, he called it. Not an unusual condition. George Bush had it when he swooned at a state dinner over in Japan. My older brother had had bouts of it, too. The doctor gave me some slowdown pills and felt confident the condition would correct itself. But he did warn: if I couldn't get it under control, I might well end up with a stroke.

Thanks, Doc. I was furious. I'm not medically-oriented. I hate hospitals and all that goes with them. But now I was putting myself on the conveyor belt run by guys with white coats and stethescopes, and everything they said scared me even more. What if this, what if that? I must have been doing something wrong, but what the devil was *causing* it? When the damnable arrythmia didn't go away, I took a stress test. Utah Jazz basketball players can run 12 minutes on the damn torture track. Most old farts like me drop off at 2 or 3. I made it to 9. Not a thing wrong with my heart. So why did I still hurt? Why was my breath so short that I couldn't walk fifty yards without having to stop?

When duck season started, I had to slog one day through a mile of marsh. The world of mountains and beauty that I loved so much began to swim in front of my eyes. I longed to be able to quit and have somebody haul me out of the bog. The active life I'd led seemed to be coming to an end.

Teddy reassured me. She said it was just the altitude up in Wyoming. At that time, we had another ranch in California. When we got back down there to warm sun and low altitude, she was certain that I'd start feeling better. I love to hunt quail. The first afternoon I drove out into the golden hills with my dogs, they located a covey not a hundred yards from my truck. I almost had to drag myself over to the birds. By the time I got there, they were gone.

We were now getting serious about the problem. Which doctor would we try? Our local fellow, who was younger than my sons, or give the pros up at Stanford a shot at it?

The next day, a curious thing happened. Because we'd been away for four months, our second class mail had stacked up. Teddy was sorting through it, picking out what we might want to read and chuck the rest in the burn barrel. Why was it that from a mound of unread periodicals, her eyes happened to strike a review of a book? The title:"Power vs. Force."

Its author was a David R. Hawkins, MD, PhD. At Columbia-Presbyterian Hospital in New York, he'd had at one time the largest psychiatric practice in the U.S. He'd also co-authored a book with Nobel Laureate Linus Pauling, had been a medical adviser for Bill Wilson, founder of Alcoholics Anonymous and had earned a PhD in Chaos Theory.

Then, moving to the Arizona desert, Hawkins had set up an institute to study the almost uncharted realm of human consciousness.

The review I was reading was in <u>Brain-Mind Bulletin,</u> a scientific journal. Its editor, Marilyn Ferguson, had written "The Aquarian Conspiracy," a best-selling herald of the New Age. Two paragraphs lept off the page:

"Dr. Hawkins has evolved what he calls The Map of Consciousness. The Hidden Determinants of Human Behavior. His 25 years of research have led him to the radical principle that our consciousness instinctively knows truth from lies, and manifests this knowledge in our bodies.

"If he's right, we could be much closer than we think to comprehending everything ftom the failings of public policy to each individual's place in the universe."

I was stunned. Could this be true, and if so, how did he know it?

Using a science called kinesiology--- testing your muscle response to ideas you hold in your mind---Hawkins has calibrated emotions according to their electrical energy. He and his assistants have tested thousands of people with kinesiology in many countries. Whether they're male, female, rich, poor or from many different races, the results are uniform. When the body hears a lie, the muscles go weak. It rejects it.

The low-end emotions of what Hawkins calls "The Box," are all negative, death-enhancing energies. They bear the electrical minus sign, starting with Death at 0, then upwards to Shame -20, Guilt -30, Apathy -50, Grief -75, Fear -100, Desire -125, Anger -150, Pride -175.

The entry point to life enhancing energies is the emotion of Courage. Here, the current of our attractor fields (electrical habit patterns) turns positive. Courage tests at +200. Then upward: Neutrality, +250. Willingness, +310, Acceptance +350, Reason +400, Love +500, Joy +540, Peace +600, Enlightenment +700.

If we live in these "top of the box" energies, we take back our power from "out there" and use it "in here" to heal ourselves.

I couldn't totally absorb what I'd read, but my body believed *something*. It seemed to *know* what Hawkins meant. I felt instantly better.

I walked outside, took a deep breath and stretched in the sun. Teddy followed me. I turned to her. "I'm not having the heart problem anymore," I said. "It's over. Finished."

She frowned. "But you don't know that. You can't be sure."

"I must have been living some kind of a lie. That's what my body is trying to tell me. If negative emotions are causing my heart to act up, then I'd damn well better dig into 'em and toss 'em out. It started in my head, so that's the place I've got to cure it."

As we sat in the patio in the sun, we replayed what had happened during the last months. Clearly, though unwittingly, I'd allowed myself to plunge into the low-end emotions. The powerful electrical attractor fields of old bad emotional habits had pulled me down until I was living in the bottom of the box.

The cause, as always, was an exterior one. It was my emotional reaction to an event "out there" that I was trying to use force to control, but couldn't.

Shortly before my heart flashed its warning, I'd published a new novel, Frontiers. Its hero was an Irish immigrant, fighting all the American wars from the Sioux in 1876 to the Japanese in 1941. He literally crossed all the frontiers of recent American history, from the plains to the oceans to the world. I never dreamed in writing it that these hundreds of pages would hurl me across my own frontier of consciousness.

It was my 13th book, years in the writing, and more or less my tour de force. I had high hopes for it. Film studios were talking about it as a miniseries. My publisher was enthusiastic, but didn't have the money to promote the book. When it hit the public, it was not with a bang but a whimper. Sales were slow. In the mass of other well-promoted books, we didn't get reviews.

Nobody knew the book was out there. We died on the vine.

As the realization struck me, I was literally heart-broken, but couldn't admit it. Instead, I hammered out a critical essay on what was wrong with the United States. Though some of the points were valid enough, nobody wanted to publish the piece. I became even more angry at the rejection I felt.

My emotional rollercoaster that I didn't know I was riding rocketed me all the way down to Shame. I was raised to be a competitor, a money-earner, but now all I had was ashes. Then Guilt. Failing to bring home the bacon, I had no sense of worth. Next came Grief. I'd worked awfully hard for a long time, thousands of pages of tries and failures. So I began mourning the past. Then Fear seized me, terror of the future. Maybe I'd never get another book published. My career was over. I was being exposed as a failure. But I couldn't let it lie there. Desire kicked in. Goddammit, I want to win! Anger now! I'll show you sonsofbitches in publishing and films! And finally, the last emotion in the bottom of the box, Pride! Tell myself I'm better than that! I deserve more!

What I was really doing was telling my heart to respond to negative programming. When you live in the low-end emotions, they always bunch up on you. You don't just act out Shame or Fear or Pride, you haul in a cluster of emotions. Your whole baggage pulls you down.

In my case, some doctor-programmed medical loop terrified me that I might have something wrong with my heart.

Consciousness, naive and trusting as a child, had to believe the program put into it. So when I inserted the negative-energy floppy disks of Guilt, Fear and Pride, consciousness sent that message down my acupuncture /meridians. Find a weakness, find some medical scare that consciousness thinks I want my body to act out. Heart seemed a likely place, being broken already. The message races down and blows the heart meridian. My body thinks that's what I want it to do, because consciousness had given such an order.

So I get the heart flutters, feel lousy and scared. Then, out of the blue, Teddy exposes me to Hawkins. Just from reading the *review* of his work, my body knew what I'd done. It saw the lie I was living.

The next step was up to me. I had to make a leap to Courage, positive energy. Courage is truth. It overpowers the darkness, the lie and the self-hate of the past. Courage tells you you can face, cope and handle. That very day, I said to Teddy, "the heart's over." It was. I'd put a new program into the computer and cancelled out the old one.

But the process was only beginning. To get higher into healing, I had to go to Neutrality. This means I would take no position. If my book makes it, fine, if it doesn't, that's okay, too. Something else will come along.

Then to Willingness. Here, I'm willing to commit myself to living in the high emotions. Make it my constant motivation. Fail and climb back up. Then to Acceptance. Surrender my will to the greater will. Whatever happens, I accept. Then to Reason: face it, I'm in my seventies in a tough business, I've never been Hemingway, what did I expect anyway? Big deal. Get real.

Then to love: "Essential for recovery," Hawkins says, "is compassion for one's self and for all of humankind. We become healers as we are healed." Charity begins at home. Now to Joy. Seeing the Oneness, having the serenity of it. Everything's perfect just as it is. From there to Peace. Bliss, no cares. And finally to Enlightenment, so far above us that it seems unreachable. But others have reached it. The constant trying is all that counts.

The genius of Hawkins <u>Power vs Force</u> is so subtle and electrifying, so foreign to us that we don't "get it" at first. How can it be otherwise? We've been raised to be competitive, controlling "winners." But he's talking about surrender to forces in our consciousness that we don't even know we know.

'Healing,' he says, 'only occurs in the higher levels of consciousness. To rise up to them most often requires struggle, despair and only through a painful surrender. Out of defeat comes victory, out of failure success, out of humbling, true self esteem.

'We may choose to no longer be enslaved by darkness.'

This was exactly the process I went through: despair over the book, defeat, and out of failure, not only surrender and humbling, but the victory of true self-esteem.

When we live in the low-end emotions, we give our power away, trying to control events "out there." In the failure of the book, I wanted to force control of something beyond my control. Hence, our satisfaction is never here, now, this moment. It's always something that might happen tomorrow or next month, something dependent on someone or something else. We live in wantingness. We have to use force to try to get our way. When we fail, we sicken.

However, when we live in the high-end emotions, we switch to positive electrical energy. We take back our power from trying to control others or events "out there" and we begin using it "in here," in ourselves. Instead of living in wantingness and constantly postponing our satisfaction, we begin living in havingness. In this-moment-now, we already have what we want. We are already "there." This is our power that heals us.

It was four years ago when Teddy and I sat in the sun and exposed the cause of my problem. From that day to the present, my heart has never missed a beat.

Why?

Could a stranger's words alone have healed me? Or was there something far more astounding here? Had I, for reasons I didn't yet understand, been suddenly lifted to a new level of consciousness?

Unwittingly, I seemed to have stumbled onto the same mysterious power that had dropped Teddy into my lap. It had let me find her in the middle of a war, then lose her when my book blew up, only to find her again.

Hadn't the same thing happened with my heart problem? Just when I seemed to have no solution for it, what power had led Teddy to pick up one review of a book out of a stack of unread mail, and happen to hand that exact one to me?

Blind luck, fate, God's will?

No. Probably all of them wrapped up in the same enigma.

What had caused me to give up control, finally let go and let God?

In some process that I knew but didn't know I knew, I must have tapped in to the synchronicity of consciousness.

How could I do it again? Could any of us? What path would we have to take so that you and I could live in it as much as possible, and pray that it would change our lives as it had changed mine?

So the search began. The quest for certainty, in a mystery that had none. Only "hints and guesses" as Eliot said, from here on in. Dark, light. Pelelieu, Paradise. Which?

Finding and losing and finding again.

And finally, God willing, the choosing between.

3.

On a morning years ago, I was out at sea off the coast of Florida, doing a movie called <u>Cinerama Holiday</u>. I'd written it and was now producing the American sequences. The Navy had given us an aircraft carrier, the Blue Angels stunt team and our very own drone airplane, a Grumman F6F that we'd shoot down in a blaze of glory as the finale of the picture.

To set all this up had taken months of negotiation with the Navy. Yes, the Cold War was going on, the Pentagon delighted to display our newest killing toys, but I wanted so much stuff for the finale the admirals soon wished they'd never heard of show business. To give our audience the thrill of hitting a carrier deck at 130 knots, we chopped off the nose of a jet and put our three-eyed monster camera into it. Aerodynamically abused, the jet kept trying to stall out, and when that ploy didn't work, it refused to put down its landing gear. We almost had to ditch it in the Atlantic before the brave pilot stalled it with such force that he snapped down the gear and came in for a heart-stopping landing. We'd also put another hardy volunteer into the ocean, to show how a helicopter could winch him up. By the time we'd set up the shot, the poor kid was so frozen he could barely hold onto the rescue sling.

However, after all the snafus, on a bright, sunny morning off of Jacksonville, the day of the finale had arrived. I was standing on the bridge with the skipper of the carrier, arranging by radio the proper positions for our destroyer escort, then the screaming fly-by of the Blue Angels, and at last, the drone F6F being guided to its death by its mother plane far above.

But first, it was vital that we rehearse the scene. We had millions of dollars of hardware about to go into the drink, and all the ducks had to be in a row. No second chances. My cameraman was down on the flight deck manually panning the bulky three-lens Cinerama camera. As the drone plane paralleled the ship, I gave the order and the carrier's 3 and 5 inch guns began to fire.

Beautiful, billowy white bursts ranged in a few practice yards behind the drone.

Delighted with the trial run, I crackled down to the cameraman: "Okay with you, Harry?"

"Sheeit!" he crackled back. We had no zoom lens on the camera. "All I'm seeing is a fuckinay little butterfly out there. Get that admiral to bring it in within a hundred yards of the ship or we'll lose the goddamn thing!"

Now we had a problem. Of course the Cold War was raging, military budgets were unquestioned, vital to our freedom, but, as the admiral wearily pointed out, "If I bring it in that close, it could go out of control and kamikaze the carrier." Did I know what a kamikaze was? I said, Yes, I'd had the pleasure of some at Okinawa. Didn't I realize I was asking him to risk his carrier and his career?

I must have ducked it some way. He sulked a moment, then sighed on the radio to the mother plane: "Bring the aircraft in to within a hundred yards of the ship, not one inch closer!"

As they say in the war movies, this is it. My heart was in my throat, the cameraman barking at me: "Have 'em hit it directly amidships, right opposite me." I relayed it to the gun crews, the bluejackets twisting their knobs, FIRE!, the bursts popping cotton in the sky, blasting yards behind the plane, getting the range for the moment of the kill.

BLAMMO! Exactly in the right place, the drone blew up, arched into a crippled split-S and exploded in a spectacular geyser.

A thousand sailors on the deck began to cheer, flinging their hats into the air. I raced from the bridge down to the flight deck and threw my arms around the cameraman.

His face was ashen. "Harry," I said, "something wrong?"

"I didn't get it," he groaned.

He'd been so fascinated watching the glorious bursts of freedom he'd forgotten to pan the camera!

The rockets red glare, the bombs bursting in air. Amen, amen, somebody up there must have heard. Days later, when we screened the footage in New York, the Grumman managed to splash into the sea about three inches from the edge of the screen.

When the producer saw the shot, he pursed his lips and sighed. "Take your crew down to Annapolis. We'll end the picture with the Navy choir singing a hymn."

Ending war with peace. That's what consciousness is, yours and mine, and "I Didn't Get It" is the operative line, the mystery of it.

Every one of us has a consciousness ---for one simple reason.

It's our human spirit. It's born into us.

But you don't know where it's flying. Ever. You just think you've got it on camera, you've nailed it amidships right where you live, and then in the next moment, the damn thing slithers away and disappears almost off your screen.

Consciousness is our common dream. Mark Twain tapped into it, I think, when he said, "You are the maker of the dream."

The choice is ours. Do we use consciousness to lift ourselves high enough into enlightenment to make the dream of our lives come true? Or do we allow our baser emotions to trap us forever in the darkness?

Whatever we call it---luck, karma, synchronicity or God's will---the dream thought we hold of our lives has immense energy. In some ethereal and barely understood process, positive thoughts and healing emotions seem to rocket us into a higher level of existence. Good things happen to happen because, in effect, we've said yes to them. We've trusted. Given up control.

But to tap into your consciousness by living in your higher emotions is a dicey thing. Where do you start? Where are the bootstraps to pull yourself up?

One moment you see clearly what your nobler instincts are telling you to do. You're dancing in the blinding white light of grace. And the next moment, it's all dark and gone. Finding and losing and finding again. You think you know how to do it, you're rising up into a happy, pleasant space and then---whammo!---some event "out there", some tug from the past flings you back down onto the floor, back to grubbing around in sad and seamy things. You've done something you don't want to do, and don't know why you did it.

That's the sticker shock in consciousness. Your emotions control it. We are what we think. The thoughts we hold in our heads trigger emotions. If we think love or joy for the dream, or think hate and anger for doom, our bodies and our very lives will eventually act them out.

Our consciousness is totally naive. It's the magical limitless child in us that knows no time or space. It is us before we were us with a body or a name. In its utter trust, it believes anything we tell it. If we want Mark Twain's dream, it says, "Fine, go to it, lass or lad. I'll make your human container give you just that because you ve told me it's what you want."

"But if doom's your thing, to wallow in grief, apathy and self-hate, help yourself, my friend. You've told me you want it, and I'm so naive, I not only trust and believe you, but I'll start right now to make your body give you your precious doom."

Think of yourself as a computer, run by electrical energy. You can program it any way you want. Bliss in, bliss out. Or garbage in, garbage out. It's your choice, your call.

What boots up your computer, starts it running, is your consciousness.

The great scientists--Jung, Einstein, Bohm, Sheldrake, Pribram and many others---have been convinced that consciousness is the incredible data base of your computer. *In it are recorded all the thoughts and all the actions of every human since the beginning of time.*

Your consciousness has been there and done that forever. It is, literally, what you don't know you know.

As neurosurgeon Karl Pribram explains it: "Based on research that goes back even pre-Einstein, we now conclude that our brains construct objective reality by interpreting frequencies that are ultimately projections from another dimension, a deeper order of existence that is beyond space or time. The brain is a hologram, enfolded in a hologrammic universe."

Another dimension beyond space or time. That's where consciousness lives. For example, imagine I'm sitting here beside you speaking these words to you. But they don 't go to you directly, say the scientists. Instead, the words I speak or write rocket up into consciousness like a radar beam, and then

22

rocket back down to you.

Consciousness is storing our dialogue out in its overlapping holograms. It even stores our thoughts. They are an electrical energy in an attractor field and are active forever in the collective consciousness of the race.

Mystics throughout the ages have suspected this. Psychiatrist Carl Jung first named the phenomenon "the collective consciousness." Recent discoveries in particle physics, nonlinear dynamics and chaos theory all support his conclusion. Every atom of everything on earth, including thoughts, is connected to everything else.

A scientist in Los Angeles takes a cell of skin from your hand and divides it. He FedEx's half of it back to a lab in New York. A scientist there heats his half cell on a burner. In Los Angeles, a continent away, the other half of your cell registers the same heat.

Interconnectedness. You and I and every living thing are inescapably plugged into the ethereal database of consciousness.

Ridiculous?

We'd think so at first. But then, can we believe in something like x-ray or radio waves? Just because we can't see them doesn't mean they don't exist.

Surely there have been times in your life, usually unwittingly, when you've tapped into the power of consciousness.

Make the test yourself. Have you ever been struck by:

---The positive energy of certain people?

---The unexpected happening of certain events?

---The unexplained healing of certain ills?

They're all in the mysterious bundle of consciousness.

Why is it that when you're around someone who obviously lives in the lower emotions, you're apt to feel tired and drained? However, when you're with someone who lives in the higher positive emotions, you're attracted to that person's electricity without knowing why. He or she just makes you feel good and right, even freed for a moment. You have been entrained into that person's powerful attractor field.

Why is it that something happens that you can't explain?

Something drops into your lap. Usually it's for your own good, but it can be bad, too. Often it's a mixture of both. But whatever the mysterious force is, you had absolutely nothing to do with making it strike you just at that moment. Chances are you were at the end of your rope. Tied in a box, trapped. You couldn't see a way out. Then, when you least expected it, a wild idea pops into your head. Why? What put it there? Why were you *told* to do some crazy thing you'd never done before? Or why did you happen to make a wrong turn on a certain morning, walk on a different street and bump into somebody who was going to change your life? Something snapped on a Eureka light in your head. In an instant, you suddenly knew what you didn't know you knew. It all seemed planned somehow. But who was doing the planning? Who was giving you this strange rush into undreamed of creativity and freedom?

You can call it Providence as they did in the old days, or fate, or luck or just being in the right place at the right time. But who was doing the timing? Who picked the place? What electricity was running your schedule right then? If you're religious, you try calling it God's will. You're content to leave it at that, but way down deep, you know you'll never know the why of it.

Something spooky is at work here.

When you rise in consciousness, up into a more powerful attractor field, what seemed true at a lower level is no longer true, if it ever was. You re-conceptualize. The mystery of synchronicity is, when you manage to rise up into a more powerful attractor field, similar people or events seem to be attracted to you---they find you. Like attracts like. Two magnets join. You're now open to new contacts, fresh ideas. Things you never expected begin to happen. Concepts like networking arise from nowhere and become a new technique in human relations. The same for the undreamed of neural network of the Internet, mirroring the interconnectedness of consciousness itself.

The third test you can make deals with sickness and healing. Why is it that one moment you can be lying in bed with a bad cold, and when you wake up the next morning it's gone? Did Contac do it or Vicks Vapo Rub? They might have helped, probably more so if you believed in them, but something else turned off your "sick" and made you get well.

The healing power of consciousness has vast implications for you and me personally, and for the sum of us in our society. It affects our beliefs, our behaviors and the systems of our civilization.

For thousands of years, sages, mystics and saints have been able to tap into the unseen power of healing. They're at the top of the box because they've lived a constant motive of enlightenment. They've dedicated themselves to a practice of living as much as they can in the higher levels of consciousness that most of us barely know. Christ is here, Buddha, Lord Krishna and the Mother Teresas of the world.

But for the rest of us, ordinary mortals? Do we have a chance?

In his book, Hawkins writes, tongue in cheek: "Even the ape Koko at the Primate Research Center has tested at a level of 250. She's intelligent, affectionate and trustworthy, meaning that one is safer with Koko than with 85% of the humans on the planet."

Throughout the ages, his testing has shown that humanity's level of consciousness has stood at a perilous 190. Then, in 1986, unaccountably, it jumped to 205. He sees this as hope. Awareness is spreading, perhaps through the proliferation of self-help groups like AA and a consciousness-raising wave that appears to be sweeping across society. These people are seeking truth, about themselves and their world.

Yet we're a long way from "getting there," healing ourselves en masse. It only happens with increments of humanity. Some are rising, others are plunging deeper into negative behaviors which, more than often, are mirrored in the structures we make. If we live in fear, we build fortresses of fear in which to hunker down and defend ourselves. If 85% of humanity still lives in the low-end emotions, think what effect that has on our politics, business, war and society in general. The Drug War, for instance, is motivated primarily by the negative emotions of Shame, Fear and Anger. To heal effectively, it would have to rise to the level of Acceptance.

"The paradox of our puritanical society,' Hawkins says, 'is

that it encourages constant seduction but denies satisfaction: a perpetual frustration of normal outlets finds release in perverse ones."

For example, look at the effect of violence on our emotions. People tested kinesologically while viewing a fairly typical 1 hr. TV serial suffered muscle weakness 113 times in a single episode. Each time various forms of mayhem or killing were shown, the immune system was weakened and a disruption of the acupuncture system occurred, supressing the thymus gland and damaging the neurohormonal and neuro-transmitter systems.

For this reason, Hawkins reports from his clinical experience, "drug-users who listen to heavy metal rock have a zero recovery rate. Its meaning is death. So too the video games where kids push the buttons and destroy screen monsters. The lesson is kill-kill-kill."

He believes that 85% our physical ills are caused by our living in the low-end emotions. "Subtle grades of depression kill more people than all other diseases of mankind combined. *There is no anti-depressant that will cure a depression that is spiritually based, because the malaise does not originate from brain dysfunction but from an accurate response to the desecration of life.* The body is a reflection of the spirit in its physical expression, and its problems are the dramatization of the struggles of the spirit which gives it life. Everyone dies by his or her own hand. That's not a moral view, but a clinical fact."

His method of healing is dramatically simple. It's the understanding, that what we hold in our mind will eventually manifest itself in our body. Our naive consciousness believes anything it sees on a billboard or hears in a TV commercial. It believes a fear-inducing medical news story, or a well-intentioned but terrifying comment from a doctor. Unless we cancel out that negative program by a positive one, our consciousness is going to tell our body to give us such an affliction. It thinks we want it because that's the program we put in.

Suppose at an early age we've heard some relative say, "Oh, we have allergies in our family." The loop is now in our consciousness. Sooner or later, in some period of stress, we develop allergies. Same thing for heart, stroke, cancer. We program them into our consciousness, and our body leads us in the direction we've accepted.

Hawkins has cured many life-threatening diseases in himself, and has surrounded himself with others who have cured cancer, stroke, diabetes, etc. His method is this: you re-program your consciousness. You don't name a symptom like, say, cancer or migraine. You simply say to yourself: "I used to believe my head had to ache or my lungs had to be poisoned. But now I know I'm an infinite being, perfectly loved by God, and I'm not subject to those conditions anymore. I don't believe them. I cancel them."

What you've done is to replace a negative emotional program with a positive one. You've taken the first leap up out of the bottom of the box. Now you're in Courage. Yes, I can face, cope and handle this. From there, with consistent motivation and repeated cancelling, you slowly move upward into the higher healing energies of love and compassion.

By such canceling, in Hawkins' own case, sometimes his symptoms would leave instantly. Other conditions took longer, even a year or two of repeated daily canceling, but eventually, they all left him. Having worn glasses since he was 14, he finally cancelled the need for them, surrendered his "blindness" to God, and much of his sight was restored.

He also feels it's difficult but possible for anyone to reach the higher levels. Motivation is the key. Motivate yourself to live up there. Forgive yourself when you fall back into the bottom of the box. You're only human, and you have to accept and love your humanness. For instance, say you plunge down into Anger. All right, get mad, feel your anger.

Somebody crosses you, acts like a real stinker, or some piece of machinery like a computer crashes and breaks your agenda into pieces. It's a perfectly neutral event out there, but you take it personally. You curse it, you punch it, you give it the finger. You've never acted like that in your life, but here you are howling and dancing around like a crazy little monkey! It's fun! You really enjoy losing it! But after a few seconds, you say to yourself: "Hey, this is not me. I don't live down here in anger. I just visited it momentarily."

So you train yourself to realize that the low-end emotion is not you anymore. You become simply a neutral observer, watching a comical little monkey-person acting out pure humanness, and forgiving it instantly because it's just our condition to fall into these lower emotions. But now, by detaching, seeing their comedy, we can even get a chuckle out of them. We've removed ourselves from the self.

"Kinesiology," Hawkins says, "the testing of our muscle response to thoughts we hold in our minds, is simply a tool. It's our window into what we haven't been aware of before."

Our consciousness is our human spirit. We can call it God or Buddha or Mohammed or the Life Force, but it is what runs us. We express it through our emotions. The theory of using our higher emotions to heal ourselves is certainly not unique to David Hawkins. In fact, it reflects the perennial philosophy of the ancient sages who identified the levels of spiritual growth we must ascend on our ladder to enlightenment. In various forms, such modern healers as Dossey, Chopra, Pert, Weil, Moore and Caroline Myss are all on the same theoretical wave length. They've recognized the power of consciousness and are teaching people how to tap into the vital life force of their souls.

We all want a brave new world, personally and for our nation, but it appears we'll never have it until we remake our own new worlds inside. As Tolstoy put it: "Everybody thinks about changing humanity. Nobody thinks about changing himself."

The question is: how do you do it? Where do you begin your journey up out of darkness?

On some level, whether we admit it or not, we're all looking for peace. We long to live, as much as humanly possible in the love, joy and peace of enlightenment.

If this is true, then why do we give so much of our spirit to getting and spending, worrying, craving, coddling our ego image until invariably it hurls us back down to T.S. Eliot's "garlic and sapphires in the mud"---grubbing around in self-made darkness?

Must our human nature do this to us? Are we doomed to being part angel and part beast, and never knowing which is running our show?

Or could our state of wantingness be culturally induced? If the society we live in has indoctrinated us to darkness, brainwashed us into believing that this is the natural state of affairs and all we can be within it---having no way to escape our tribal thinking---then doesn't it make sense to see how that thinking became so deeply rooted in us, and how we can cast it out and begin all over again?

You have to go back to where you've been, before you can see where have to go.

4.

A few months after I'd been exposed to Hawkins' thinking, consciousness zapped me with another bullet of truth. It wasn't an e-mail but rather a c-mail, appearing without warning in my computer's In-box.

A local woman's club had asked me to give a speech. This is standard operating procedure for writers. I was flogging my Frontiers novel which at the time was still as hidden from the public as a state secret. So I was eager to talk about it to anybody who'd listen. The ladies told me to lug up some copies under my arm, they might even buy a few.

What they really wanted, unfortunately, was less about the book and more about the curious life a writer must lead. Who were these strange ducks, and why in the world was one hiding out back in the hills of San Benito County, California? In short, don't you meet the most fascinating people? Drop some names, enchant us with a few funnies while we're digesting lunch, and then let us go back to real world where actual people live.

As a natural procrastinator, I put off until the last minute preparing what I was going to say. Then, unaccountably, I happened to reach across the litter of my desk and picked up the same copy of Brain-Mind Bulletin where I'd stumbled onto David Hawkins. Now, this didn't have anything to do with Hawkins or me, but in a story on a different page, one line caught my eye.

"Happiness is less a matter of getting what you want than wanting what you have."

Hmm, I thought, that has a nice ring. The writer was a psychologist named David Myers. I'd heard the idea expressed in various other ways, so I didn't think he'd mind if I borrowed his rendition. I'd use it as filler, a throw-away transition from one part of the speech to the next.

I hurried out of my office at the ranch and drove north for an hour to the mid-sized town that was our county seat. There were few cars on the road up, and only an occasional calf that had crawled through a fence somewhere and was wandering, bleating for his mother. Leisurely I jotted on a palm-sized card a few lead lines about some funny incidents that had happened to me on the way to the final page.

When I arrived at the small town restaurant and met the ladies, I had a sweet vermouth to warm up. Then came the chicken and peas lunch, the pledge of allegiance, and I stood up to start talking. I began with the mandatory opener joke, then used the shot-down Grumman on Cinerama as the symbol of a writer's life: you see a beautiful story out there, and in the end have to groan: "I didn't get it." The ladies' response was a faint chuckle or a groan. Clearly, they weren't getting much of it thus far. I was even thinking of throwing in Teddy falling down the stairs, but instead, groping for a transition, I tossed out the borrowed line:

"Happiness is less a matter of getting what you want than wanting what you have."

It was as if I'd flung a hand-grenade into the room. Here now I was talking about *them*, not merely spooling out my own funnies. These women weren't fancy or sophisticated. They were wives of ranchers, farmers, secretaries, local business owners. Grass-roots people, innately shy, yet now their eyes whipped to me. A few clapped, others cried, "Yes! That's true!"

I was stunned. The response was almost electric, as if the words "*wanting what you have*" had sparked something they knew but didn't know they knew. When they heard it, they responded in a reflex of instant agreement.

Wasn't it proof of what Hawkins was saying? Where shall we live, in wantingness or in havingness? Our bodies instinctively knew the difference between lie and truth.

The rest of the speech, at least to me, was an anti-climax. I think I sold a book or two but clearly the ladies were interested in their own happiness, not the fiction of someone else's. As I was leaving, one rugged old gal with henna hair gripped my hand. "Wantin' what you have, eh? You said somethin' there, mister!"

All the way home, down through the golden hills, the

vineyards and steep brushy rangeland, I pondered what had happened.

Obviously these women, like you and me, were seeking the truth about the meaning of our lives.

As Americans, we've believe in getting. Happiness is getting what we want. To do so, we've been trained to compete, to control. These ordinary small-town women were no more avaricious than anyone else, in fact, probably less so because they lived outside the mainstream. Yet few of us can escape the influence of our culture. In myriad ways, desire has been hot-wired into us. Wantingness. Wanting something out there that somebody must give us, and if not, we have to use force to get it. Our schools, government, media and families relentlessly teach us that our purpose in life is to win. We're in a war. Victory is beating the system so that it showers on us our fair share of money, power, fame or possessions. These are clearly the rewards our society reveres. If you get them, you're a winner. You're somebody. You're worth something.

If you fail to get them, you're a loser. Nobody. Occupant. No worth as a human being.

But my few random words struck down this cultural lie. Instinctively, the womens' bodies *knew* that our belief system of getting has brought us only flashes of happiness against a darkening sky of increasing disillusionment.

Millions of us suffer from actual or imagined physical ills. We're the most medicated people on earth, yet few of us heal.

An estimated three-quarters of us mistrust our government. Less than half of us even vote. Despite a currently robust economy and soaring stock market, a strange feeling of unease persists. For many of us, our system doesn't seem to be working. Our traditional values are eroding. We don't quite know where we are or how we got there. More and more we feel depersonalized. We respond to the desecration of our lives in fear, doubt and rage, yet we don't know what to do about it.

As a people accustomed to getting our way---winning---it appears that we have tried to force our will on ourselves and our nation. When we fail, when nothing changes, we feel powerless. By trying to control events out there, over which we have no control, we have lost our power in here, in ourselves.

If our mind is an electrical energy like a computer, these women and I were programming ourselves with software of the past or the future. We were grieving about what we didn't get yesterday, or we were fearing what we might not get tomorrow.

We were making our happiness conditional on people or events that had been or will be. Thus, we had cut ourselves off from the only true happiness any human can ever know: to live in this moment right now.

Why do we do this to ourselves?

Because we are what we think, what we hold in our minds. We are governed by our emotions. When we live in the low-end emotions of guilt, apathy, grief, fear, desire, anger and pride, our bodies know that we're living in wantingness. We're perpetually unfulfilled. Our electrical energy goes negative, we suppress our immune systems, we sicken, we die.

However, when we live in the high-end emotions, courage, neutrality, willingness, acceptance, reason, love, joy and peace, our bodies know that we're living in havingness. We're fulfilled. In this moment now we already have everything we need. It's "in here" with us. We create our own happiness. Our electrical energy goes positive. Our immune systems respond. We heal, we live.

Our cultural lifestyle of wantingness is a dead end. We never get "there" because, as Gertrude Stein said, "there is no there there." "There" is forever dependent on someone else or some event giving us something in the future. We never get enough of what we want, whether it's money, power, fame or things. Thus, we rob ourselves of the precious moment of the present, the exact now where we can discern truth and what we really are.

The result?

Lives of quiet desperation. Distracted from distraction by distractions. Play catch up ball. Smile the smile of friendly unhappiness. Have a nice day. Make my day. Get a life.

When we can't control the "out there," can't get our way, we as individuals and nation respond in frustration, fear and sickening. Our wantingness has given us a century of failed systems and crushed souls.

Our bodies have been reacting by reflex to the lie we are living. Our emotions are responsible for imprisoning us in the darkness of wantingness. The media, particularly advertising, has swamped us with Desire. Our rising expectations are usually forever unfulfilled. But the leap to Courage requires us to face the truth about ourselves, own up to our weakness, neediness and inflated self-images that are all the common clay of human behavior. Admit them, forgive them and go on. Should enough of us re-program ourselves to live in the higher emotions of havingness, isn't it possible that by healing ourselves, we might also begin to heal our nation?

When I got home, Teddy asked me how the speech went. "Hawkins all over again," I said. "Like the song, 'Everywhere I go, sunshine follows me.'" Then I had to smile. "The reaction of those ladies told me one thing for sure. I seem to have been living in wantingness all my life."

"Everybody does, darling."

"But do we have to?" I shook my head. "There's got to be a book in this---if I can just figure out how to tell it."

"You will," she said. "Take the ego out of it and surrender to it. It'll come."

Surrender! What an alien concept to Americans, and certainly to me at that moment. Yet the leap to courage, to the positive electricity of healing emotions---wasn't that the beginning point of surrender?

You'd be saying to yourself, "No matter what nasty stuff life throws at me, I'm resolving in this moment to face, cope and handle it." That's courage, and the surrender is, you do your best and forget the outcome. It's the end of "I know." It's the admission that I don't know, and to heal myself, I trust consciousness to show me the better way.

How different this was from our normal approach to life. I thought of my years of political writing, the outpouring of facts, figures, ideals, the pretensions that I *knew* The Way. Like any other good citizen, loyal believer in the American Dream, I'd put my trust in politics. I'd delude myself that if we could only elect the right president, the country would turn around. We'd settle our differences. If the economy improved, the tide would lift all boats. If we could be kinder and gentler, we'd lessen our crime, hate and violence. If we had better education, our people would become wiser, more responsible citizens. If we wait for the next medical wizardry, somebody will come up with a cure for cancer, AIDS, broken-heartedness and depression. If we go to church more, if we pray, won't our present despair go away and we'll live happily ever after?

But the power the women and I touched in that room had nothing to do with any of the above. What our bodies have known forever and Hawkins and many other scientists are now corroborating---we already have the power. It's our consciousness--- universal and accessible to every one of us: an infinite database containing all the electrical energy of all the thoughts and all the behaviors of mankind since the beginning of time.

The truth it demands from us *is* a leap to courage, because courage is the turning point where we can begin to use our power "in here," in ourselves. Stop draining away our energy in the darkness of negative emotions. Live in the positive ones and rise toward the light that will set us free.

In the war of wantingness, seek victory no more, but only now surrender---to the peace of havingness.

Give up your war, it says.

But could I? Could you, or any of us?

5.

You've been raised on war. All of us have had a heavy dose of it in our 20th century of war. It doesn't much matter whether it's actual killing someplace out in the world, or just the mock killing you have to do in your business life or in your sports. Somebody has to win, somebody has to lose.

When I was a boy, it seemed much simpler. I thought war meant shooting people, and after enough had bit the dust, you captured their flag and declared victory.

We had a grand arsenal to do it with. For real-life war games, we usually played on bikes, swooping past each other with cap guns popping, water pistols dousing and home-made machine guns stinging the enemy with rubber bands. If the weather was too bad to play outside, we did our wars with lead soldiers, of which we had uncounted regiments. When their rifles got too bent or their heads came off, we heated up lead and molded our own replacement troops, painting them splendidly in the uniforms of the day. We could choose any war we wanted, everything from jousting with our knights to the gallant boys in Blue and Gray being scythed down at Gettysburg. We had scarlet-coated British colonials fighting seedy-looking Boers, we had Spahis, Chasseurs Alpins and the horrible fuzzy-wuzzies of Omduran. A favorite annihilation was noble Custer being pincushioned by the savage Sioux.

But back then in the 1920's, the war we loved best was still echoing in our ears. The Big One, the war to end wars. Our fathers had fought in it. They brought home their tales, saucy French jokes and gas masks fogged with disillusion. We didn't catch that part of it, though. Instead, we dug trenches in our sandbox and had our swaggering doughboys rise up to swarm over the hated Huns.

Then, on a night in 1931 when I was nine years old, my father, Roy, came into the darkened bedroom where my brother Bill and I were sleeping. "Bad news, boys," he said gravely.

"Just heard it on the radio. The Japs are marching into Manchuria. Sure as shooting, they're going to get us into a war."

His words sounded like something I might hear in a movie, and they terrified me. I didn't know what a Jap was. If there were any on the north side of Chicago where we lived, I'd never seen one. As for Manchuria, which Roy said was someplace near China, it was too far away to have any meaning for me.

Then he told us briefly about the League of Nations, what a great dream it was, but now the Japs were killing it for good by pulling out. He shook his head and blew a hissing little breath through his teeth. I'd seen him do this so often during the Depression years.

After he'd left us, Bill and I lay staring at the shadows crossing the ceiling, headlight beams of a last few automobiles out on Sheridan Road. When Bill finally went off to sleep, I couldn't. I got up out of bed and sat shivering at the window, looking down into the courtyard of the apartment. The Japs, I knew, would come sneaking in here, no lights, nobody would see them. Like monkeys, they'd scale their way up the big window ledges, apartment by apartment, until they reached ours on the third floor. Then what?

Though I was deathly afraid, I longed for them to come. We were playing war all the time, weren't we? Now I had to see for myself what a real one would be like. I knew my father dreaded war, but on the other hand, he had so many books and films about it, he must have loved it, too.

Was it good or bad, and which part of it did I want?

I fell asleep at the window, wondering if I even had a choice.

About then, another aspect of life was beginning to dawn on me. We were raised as Catholics. My mother, the eldest of 13 children, was particularly devout. My father, Roy, was perhaps less so, but he gave generously to the church, even if he sighed and dozed through most of the sermons. So my path, early on, was made clear. First Communion, later Confirmation, march all the steps upward to sanctity. Mother sent me to a nearby Cenacle convent where pious Sister Margaret Mary instructed me ever so gently in all the rotes and rites. I memorized the Catechism and when I didn't miss a word of it, she'd drop a marshmallow into

38

my cocoa cup.

Finally, the big day arrived when I would actually receive the Host. I was overjoyed, cleansed, freed. After the priest put the wafer on my tongue, I whirled, and when I reached Sister in one of the rear pews, she was smiling. "Oh, you angel," she said. "Do you realize, you were skipping all the way down the aisle?"

"I have no sins," I said.

As my reward that day, I got two marshmallows in my cocoa.

But it was out there, the sinlessness and the love. How to put it together with the fight part of me?

We didn't worry about it too much. We went back to our war games, using a little gas-powered Red Bug now as our tank, or smacking each other around on the football field. In the war play or the horsing with BB guns and later .22's, there was one strict rule, and our fathers were jumpy and stern about it: Never point any kind of gun at anybody, even in jest. It was all right to play fighting as a game, but you had to stop it there or they'd take away all our hardware and make us do homework.

A short decade later, they gave us our guns back, neat, real McCoy guns now, and told us, "Get one for me, boys." We did our best. We got some. Enough to win and declare an enormous victory. We had finally won The Big One World War Two and that was the end of it forever.

For five years anyway. Then along came a new Enemy Out There we had to destroy. Korea, Berlin Airlift, Cuba, Vietnam, Central America---endless enemies. So off we went again into the barbed wire and did the paying and the dying for the next forty-five years. When we got too old, we hired others to do it for us. It seemed as if war were something nobody could give up, even if they wanted to.

Why is it so hard? Because the shooting part is easy to be against. It's like sin. You don't want it, you've got to be against it. But it's only the smoke.

Real war is the volcano below, that time-bomb that ticks in our daily lives, building its pressure in how we think, how we act toward each other, what our goals are, until finally it reaches a boiling point and blows its top.

War in our hearts.

Just to get by and live a decent life nowadays, you run into obstacle after obstacle. Too often, your agenda lies in pieces all over the floor. Your job has gone sour, the wife is spending too much money, the kids are messes. What are you going to do? Punch out the boss, break a dish over the wife's head or cane the kids? No, usually you swallow it, and the bitterest choke-down is when you're angry at yourself for not being a winner. You have so much anger bottled up that it has to go someplace. Then along comes your neighbor and his dog digs up your lawn. Explode! Lay it on the bastard! And now on the evening news, here's a Really Bad Person over in some foreign country trying to stick it to the good old USA. They're talking about Your Country, You! Hit'im! Nuke 'im! The scapegoat becomes the container for the hate in our hearts.

But peace is also in our hearts. In the war of your life and mine, we've all seen it, touched it, longed to hold onto it, despite the world screaming at us: You can't give up your war. It's in us, it's human nature, we're stuck with it.

So you and I keep on trying to capture the flag until one day the enemy in us shoots back and fells us and our dream of winning. Our consciousness dictates terms of surrender.

The only victory you and I can seek now, if we dare to end the war in us, is just the reverse of everything we've been taught. The guns are gone, the killing over. It's a jolt, a blow, an insult to our common sense and a denial of everything we'd held dear.

Lay down our arms? Just up and quit? Who said?

Our consciousness said. War sickens, peace heals. Take your choice.

There isn't any.

Weaponless, captured, all that's left is to make the leap into the unknown. Only one thing is certain:

Getting there will not be half the fun.

Because you're never there and it doesn't matter anyway. Peace doesn't care.

All that counts is your trying,
The knowing that, at least,
You've begun.

6.

Your first break with the old thinking comes when you realize that peace is not the absence of war. Peace means filling the vacuum of war---that side of you that you're trying so hard to exorcise---filling it instead with your sacred *youness*, your uniqueness, treasuring and acting out your infinitesimal but divine role in the unfolding of all life.

You're truly one of a kind, the only model ever made like you. As an old rancher once told me about water: "Use it or lose it."

The peace you're reaching for is just as precious as water because it's your own. Nobody can tell you how to "get" it or make a buck on it. It's self-taught, this witching up the water of your soul.

Not only do you have to learn to think and live in a new way, but on a much deeper level, to re-conceptualize your whole purpose. Why have you been put here in the first place? Your life or mine: what are they all *about*, anyway?

In our befuddled era where polls tell who we are and what we think, suppose one day we gave a war and nobody came? That is, as pollsters, we interviewed the first hundred people on any street in America. We asked them a single question: "What is the meaning of your life?"

Would any one of them answer: "Enlightenment?"

I doubt if I would. I was like the drunk who'd lost his car keys and was wandering around in the darkness looking for them. When he began searching a ditch by the road, a friendly passerby said, "Did you lose your keys in that ditch?" The drunk straightened up unsteadily. "No," he said, "but there's a street light here."

Like the song of the hippie years, "Looking for love in all the wrong places," part of the lostness I felt was not knowing what spirit was, where to look for it and how to cope with it if I found it.

Like most of us, I fear, I'd had virtually no training in the search and rescue technique of putting spirit into my life. Before my heart gave me a warning, I didn't realize that my emotions were the physical acting out of the struggle of my spirit to claw its way up out of the box I'd made for it. Not until I was forced to connect the dots did I begin to understand that consciousness *is* my spirit.

Mine, yours, everybody's. Consciousness runs every single one of us---and it's a wonderwoman, a quiz kid, a logic board in our computer capable of plugging every thought and action we have into the eternity of all thoughts and actions that have ever taken place. Talk about the internet. Our consciousness-spirit is the web of the universe---with no log-on fees or line charges. We're already on line, free, every one of us. The only price we pay is the leap to courage to begin using the incredible thing.

The problem is, spirit has long been an outcast to most of us . A voice crying in the wilderness. It doesn't play by the rules of our culture. It makes no money and makes no wars. It has nothing to prove, no fortresses of fear to defend, no image to preserve. It cares passionately about the present moment, the NOW in which it lives, hurls itself into it---be careful in nothing!---and then, in surrender, does not care about any reward. To spirit, we've already had our reward, just in the courage of our trying.

And the enlightenment, the carrot at the end? It is so unreachable because we are never there. The journey, knowing that we're on it, is all that counts. Our search for our spirit is our meaning in life. All the rest is irrelevant.

No wonder you don't get that answer on a street corner on the evening news!

Most of all, you'd better not announce it at a cocktail party or you'll clear the room.

The culture that raised us has neither time nor inclination to concern itself with the spirit. You can't blame it. Culture has work to do. The business of America is business. It's getting the cows in and the corn out. A busy, vibrant society can only occupy itself with the things it believes count: doing, chasing, getting. Spirit may moan, "There's more to life than just the chase," but then the subway doors slide shut, and you've gotta get that train! Go for the jugular of life! The game pays off on win!

So how do you swim upstream against such thinking? To put spirit into your life, you're going to have to dare to be different, jump into the river and flail away against the rushing current. Your culture, the hometown boys and girls who are sticking it out in their familiar groove don't want to see you go. You're a threat to all they hold dear. There's resentment against the guy who tries to cut with the tribe. You might find something they haven't. You're questioning the certainties they live by.

In a little adobe town in Mexico, the people used to ask their priest, "Father, how do we save our souls?" Now they ask, "Why do we have to be poor?" One Mexican I knew took action. He worked very hard in his tiny field. He hitchhiked far from his pueblo to learn new techniques of farming. He taught himself to read at night, and to understand why some seeds thrived in his soil and others did not. His goal was to *sube*---to rise. His wife worked, so did his children. They were well accustomed to labor, but now they had a reason for it. Their neighbors watched them first with suspicion, then hostility. Their fields were flowering when others lay sterile. But the crowning blow came when the young Mexican brought home a tenth-hand but serviceable tractor. He would use it to bring water to them all.

The second night he had it, while he and his family were up in the mountains cutting mesquite wood, his neighbors burned the tractor, his house and everything he had.

I've heard variations of that story with the Melanesians of the South Pacific and in the tight tribal culture of the Apaches in Arizona. There's a price to pay for breaking away.

Long ago, when my spirit cried out to me that I had to uproot from the tribe and make a new life in the West, one of my oldest friends shook his head. "I give you maybe a year, maybe five, but you'll never pull it off. You'll be back."

When the reprimands of your culture strike your consciousness, and your daring to be different becomes so abhorred, your reflex is to hurl yourself down into the worm-eating, self-hating emotions of shame, guilt and fear. Your old habit patterns scream at you in terror.

Quit it! Stop this right now! You can't rip my past out of me, tear off my security blankets. They were the devil I knew! Now you're flinging me into the unknown. To what? The alleged power of surrender? That means I'm a quitter. It goes against every bone in my body. Do you honestly expect me to believe that if I just let go, give up control over outcomes, that consciousness will hand me the dream of my life on a silver platter?

But think about it a moment. Hasn't that exact process happened to you more than once? When you least expect it, something wonderful drops into your lap. You did nothing to make it happen. You just were there at the right place at the right time.

You got a c-mail from consciousness, waking you up to what you didn't know you knew, and rigging your whole game from then on.

So how do you open your soul and let your truth and your meaning back in?

The Let Go and Let God of the great saints of history comes down to a single word:

Surrender.

Give up my will, my war against myself and my world, so that Thy will shall be done.

But we can't, we won't! We haven't been trained to think surrender. As American survivors of the 20th century, we believe in winning, and what's more, we've thrived on it. We've built the most generous, productive, powerful nation in the world by using force to get our way.

But getting our way is not necessarily our happiness. We've had our victories, and they don't seem to fill us up anymore. Did they ever? Human nature is a bottomless pit of desire, of rising expectations forever unfulfilled. No wonder we feel the lack in us, the something missing out there that we never quite get.

When I was young, I used to dream of getting my first novel published. If I could just paste it up there, see it in print, then I'd live happily ever after. Well, the book came out. It was a reasonable success. Not a month later, I was eating my guts out to do it again, feeling myself a failure if I didn't.

The ego just won't be filled up, ever, and our spirit knows why. If the scientists are correct and our consciousness has stored in its overlapping holograms all the foibles of mankind throughout the ages, then there's nothing new about our predicament. It's the human condition to want, and now the drenching we get by instant communication has aggravated it terrribly. It's mimesis, monkey see, monkey do. We've got to have what the other guy has, only more so. Daily and in all forms, we're swamped by messages and examples telling us what to think, what to believe, what to get, and by the amount of our getting, the scorekeeping, we identify who we are---worthy or unworthy human beings.

The old wisdom of our spirit says: not by bread alone does man live. There's another half of us out there longing to be filled. We have to BE as well as DO. But too often our reflex is to say: Shop till you drop. Want-get-win. Not by bread alone? No way! We're going to buy out the bakery, put it on the stock exchange and make a ton.

The result is predictable and tragic. For our pottage of material gains, we have sold out our American soul by mistaking our way of living for our meaning in life.

Triggered by the instinctive reaction of our consciousness, our spirits and bodies wail for truth in the echo chamber of our emptiness.

Yet if surrender is our only true victory and the increasingly proven way of healing ourselves, why have we failed to use its power all these years? What forces in our culture have benumbed us? What shame has caused us to put our spirit in a plain brown wrapper, lest anyone catch us reading from the dirty book of our souls?

In the society that raised me---God-fearing, church-going, "respectable" people---the subject of spirit never came up. We didn't need it. Obediently we performed the rotes, the rites and the sacraments. That was enough. We gave a nod to God on Sundays, we lock-stepped to the rules of religious bureaucracy, but the why behind all of it, the gentle voice of spirit, was drowned out by the marching feet of Onward Christian Soldiers.

From the days when I was a sinless kid skipping down the first communion aisle, all the way up through the masses and sermons of the years, I felt I'd paid my spiritual dues and then some. I'd given at the office. I'd gone on retreats, read books by holy men and listened to their tapes. Though their sincerity moved me and often helped me, their message usually got lost in the medium. Too much theology, liturgy and Biblical history that seemed far removed from any of my worldly problems. I never really "got it" until I realized that my emotions were the struggle of my spirit to rise and go free.

By the time most of us started school, there seemed nobody around who knew what spirit was. Our teachers weren't aware of the emotional/consciousness connection which is only lately being explored. Besides, something so esoteric would take precious minutes away from the valuable, testable part of our curriculum: math, social studies and gym class. In addition, we'd been lock-stepped into grades where we'd compete only with people our same age. It was easier for the bureaucracy to separate us out and keep track of us this way. Spirit might yearn for all ages to go to school in the same class, so the little kids, knowing they couldn't compete with the skills of the big ones, would simply be inspired and try to emulate their excellence. But that was apparently too much wisdom for our system of learning.

When we'd been brain-deadened and de-souled enough to enter college, our spirit was a shadow memory, driven into hiding by the reason and pride of "higher education." Spirit, though a foreign object, had a ring of danger about it. It might be connected to God in some way, as if it were the pistol shot on page one of our Cliff notes. The United States had separated church and state. Legally and intellectually, we had exorcised the God idea and the preachers and potentates connected to it. In our study of history, we knew too well the bloodbaths of religious wars, and rejoiced, rightfully, that it can't happen here, thank God. The Old Boy was dead for good, and we were olly-olly-ottsen free---as we used to shout in our war games.

By then, in our educational stamp-mill, we were too dumbed down to realize that we'd shot the wrong guy. Poor God had caught it again---and it wasn't even His fault.

Wisdom, had we listened, would have told us that religion and all its "Godness" is only one possible expression of spirit. Suppose you're into fly fishing or sky diving, break-dancing or finger-painting? You're doing spirit in each of those trivial pursuits. Church doesn't have a lock on it. Spirit is anything you love and hurl yourself into, freeing your soul and letting it sing.

But it's so damn vague to get a handle on let alone hold onto. As a business executive told me, "I'm not against this spirit thing. Just show me how I can cut through all the verbiage and find a practical application for it. Use it in the company."

Out in the world where I grew up, we talked Dow Jones at our dinner parties, where the market might be heading, who shot a birdie on the 18th hole, or whose team crunched the other in Sunday's pro football. If we ever lapsed into seriousness, it was about competition, politics, business or war. Does our tribe win, or would it be the other one, the outsiders, the enemy? We talked what you DID. Your job was YOU: how much money you made, how much power or fame you had.

I fell into it like everyone else. Then one night I happened to dine with a Japanese man who had large holdings on the island of Hokkaido. His daughter had to translate for him, which she did delightfully, covering her teeth with her tiny hand in the custom of well-bred Japanese ladies. Her father had given her a diamond ring as big as my eyeball. He had also, in a little bamboo box, brought over from the Homeland his own straw broom so that he and his wife could sweep out their daughter's house.

Being slightly in culture shock, when conversation lapsed I blurted out the standard American positioning question: what exactly did Mr. Sato do?

It went through translation and came back with widened eyes: "DO?"

"Well, yes," I said, "your father's career, his business."

He smiled and said gently through his daughter, "For the past twenty years, I am engaged in the study of the spirit. You call spirituality, no?"

Ah so.

The competitive ethic and its media-induced desires had

persuaded us to believe that we can attain happiness through wantingness and getting. All we had to do was to keep buying more tickets, and one day we'd hear the fat lady sing.

Novelist William Faulkner saw it coming. In 1955, accepting the Nobel Prize, he asked: "What has happened to the American Dream? We dozed and it abandoned us, and in the vacuum no longer sound the strong, loud voices unafraid."

Spirit is an eternal longing. We didn't invent it, we don't own it, but we're stuck with it in our consciousness, and it's begging to he heard.

In my view, part of the reason we've lost our spirit is a structural thing. Our thought processes have been muddied up by what the AA people call "stinkin' thinkin'. Like the old generals, we're still fighting the last war for the world.

But ironically, in the world we're now entering, consciousness is rising everywhere at galactic speed, and with it, a new understanding and yearning for spirit.

You know it's happening. You'd like to get a ride on this great wave, and perhaps you already are. You're doing it in a personal sense, in your tiny yet vitally important re-thinking of your meaning. Why have you been put here? What's it all *about*, anyway? Is it to want, or to have? If you and I and enough of us can rise up to such a level of enlightenment, the chances seem very good that we may again become the strong loud voices, unafraid to rekindle our American soul in ourselves and our nation.

To reach that happy day, we're going to have to stop playing by the old rules.

7.

Long ago, in a speech for Ronald Reagan, I wrote a joke about a city feller asking a farmer for directions. When the farmer didn't know where any road led, the city feller finally exploded: "Then what the hell do you know?"

"I ain't lost.'[1]

But Ronald Reagan was clearly lost, that night of November 21, 1986. In confusion, he was fumbling around, trying to defend himself to the press for the Iran-Contra scandal. What did he know and when did he know it? Millions of us who watched him on TV were even more lost, as if suddenly we were in a place we didn't want to be, and didn't know how we'd gotten there.

My mind raced back to a night in 1964, Ronald Reagan, then an actor, and Nancy with whom I'd grown up, had come over to our house in Los Angeles. After dinner, Ronnie told me that the Republican power group had asked him to run for Governor of California. He was uncertain about it. Did I think he should do it? Nancy, meanwhile, had gone into our bedroom with Teddy. They sat on our big double bed and the moment was painful for Nancy. She and Ronnie loved each other. They had a wonderful life together. Why, she pleaded, did they need the garbage of politics heaped on them?

After they'd gone home that night, I told Teddy that they were such decent people, they didn't belong in politics, and would probably be torn to pieces in the jungle of it. So much for my skill as a forecaster.

Now, twenty-two years later, Ronnie had weathered two gubernatorial terms and was working on his second as President. I was watching his press conference in a New York apartment. A small group had gathered here, Republicans and Democrats alike.The men were all national names, respected leaders in banking, media, industry and government. To them, Irangate and Reagan's dismal performance were symptoms of America gone wrong.

After the disastrous press conference was over, each man made suggestions as to what he would do to get the country back on track. As I listened to these movers and shakers, men who pushed buttons and things happened, I felt dismayed. Every remedy they offered was only part of an answer. They seemed to have no overall solution, or much hope that one even existed.

If men like these didn't know a way out, then who did?

Could it be that we were too compartmentalized, too over-specialized to see the forest for the trees? Our present plight obviously couldn't be corrected by mere "fixing," by changing this department or leak-proofing that compartment.

We seemed to be looking at America in archaic terms, trying to run our lives by the two century-old left-brain thinking of Isaac Newton and Francis Bacon. To them in their time, the engine of the world was "doing." Man was put here to DO, even though his spirit was wailing at him that he was also here to BE. So they had cut us in half with their creed, insisting that to progress and prosper, we must break the whole into its parts which then we could manufacture on a production line and market to the masses.

We would make our parts into separate objects that we could control. We considered our body as a machine. The earth was a machine. If it was broke, replace the part and fix it. Get it back on the assembly line. Under this thinking and our blind allegiance to it, we were letting Newton and Bacon still rule us from the grave.

The world wasn't working their way anymore, if it ever did, except during the Industrial Revolution. The world we were now entering was crying out for its missing half, the right brain of "being" which is where the spirit lives. The new world is an holistic One where every atom is delicately intertwined into the greater system of life, and thus totally beyond our control.

Many scientists consider the earth as a living being. We can't make it into an object anymore. We can't cut it into its parts. Thus, no matter what patchwork we weave of new policies or new political candidates, we're missing the *whole* of the problem. We never reach the core of our unraveling. Our Oneness with all life is our national soul.

Our native Americans knew this and revered it. Before they killed an animal for its hide and its meat, they always begged forgiveness from the Great Spirit for removing a living thing from the All. But now, when seventy percent of us tell pollsters that our favorite "hunting" is shopping in malls, we've pretty much lost the wisdom of the ancients. We'd like to believe that it's not our fault. The stinkin' thinkin' of our acquisitive culture has done this to us. That's partly true, but on a deeper level, we *are* responsible for much of what's happening. When we stand passively on the sidelines and permit injustice, we become guilty bystanders. We fail to speak truth to power. When we actively buy into the systems, we further their soul-crushing. As a "batagorial" on the paper sacks of a California grocery chain urges: "Don't vote. It only encourages Them."

Now, Ronnie Reagan, the night he faced the press in such dismay, was a victim of the same *zeitgeist*. He'd bought into the failed system. He didn't know anyplace else to go. And thus he, like many of us, had become part of the problem. Our ship of state, our fragmented whole, seemed to be running aground. He didn't put it there by any single, personal action. The structure did, the parts-thinking we were still steering by.

I truly felt for him, which was why, over the Christmas following his press conference, I dashed him off a quick note. Saying: look, you've had the world dump in on you, first the Irangate mess and now surgeons carving on your prostate. I only want to tell you and Nancy that you're good people, you've done many good things---in short, that you're worthy human beings, far beyond this moment of political sound and fury.

A few days later, I was standing at the kitchen sink, washing dishes, my hands full of soap when the telephone rang. "I'm sitting here," Reagan said, "looking at the letter you wrote Nancy and me. I just want to tell you, Otis, how much it means to us…"

We talked a long time, much like old times, yet when we hung up, I was puzzled. Why had he called me? I was a nobody, not a member of his inner circle, not a donor, indeed, not even a Republican, for in my disenchantment about our politics, I'd rocketed from conservative to liberal and all the way out the far end to radical. Meaning one who goes back to the roots, and the one I was trying to dig up was our missing soul.

I couldn't "do" anything for Ronnie. I was just a distant friend from the past. So why had he called? Could it be, I wondered, that even in the world's most powerful job, he felt moments of loneliness and despair, exactly as all of us do. We long for somebody, anybody, to reach out and touch us. Reassure us that it wasn't all in vain, and that we were good, valuable human beings regardless of what we'd won or lost.

Didn't it come down in the end to our sense of worth? Three little words: "I love you"---win or lose. But more often now in our land, we tend to say "I hate you"---for not bringing home your share of the bacon.

Where we needed reassurance most was where we were least prepared to cope with it. In failure. What is failing is the merciless creed of our culture: do-get-win. Be Number One, be in control, be right. That's what our game paid off on, and what is causing so much anguish in our spirit.

Now surely, winning, success or the things we acquire aren't bad or a cause for guilt. They're a natural part of life, enjoyable and sometimes uplifting. But where our society muddies our thinking is when we make them into ends, into idols of themselves. Out of all proportion, they tend to become demons blinding us to our greater meaning.

Because in such obsession, when we can't win every time, when we're revealed as human and fallible, our achievements fade into bereavements. We're stricken. Failing to be approved, stroked, loved, we feel a terrible unworth, and hate ourselves for our losing.

If this could be true for a President, mightn't it even be true for a nation? Did we find ourselves so whipped by our self-inflicted creed that inevitably we must fail it because its approval-hunger is so insatiable? Despite what the ads tell us about "having it all," we can't possibly attain it, because all is never enough for the human ego and never has been.

As a result, we cast ourselves much of the time into a torment of unhappiness, a perpetually unfulfilled sense of worth. Constantly, we think we have to drive ourselves harder, play "catch up ball" to overcome our "failures" as if only by such frenzy can we get back even with the game---the dream we had once known, and felt we were still promised, but most of the time no longer knowing what it was.

When Reagan asked me to write a speech for him in his abortive 1976 presidential campaign, I titled it "God Bless America," an unoriginal plea to put our American soul back into our lives.

A few days later I received a hasty, hand-written note from him in Pacific Palisades:

"Dear Otis,

Home to pick up clean laundry and your speech--- please, my heart-felt thanks. Maybe I'll just keep it for Sunday mornings on the road when I can't get to church. I'm not joking Otis it's beautiful and will be of great value to me. Again, please accept my gratitude. I'll try to be deserving.

Ron

To my knowledge, he never used a word of the speech.

I'd written a no-no, talking about soul. For a pragmatic politician, dedicated to doing/winning, the vapory being of soul had to be anathema. Soul smacked of religion, and no politician dared mix the two. Indeed, hadn't we pretty much burned out soul in generations of faithful churching that mixed up God with religion until we thought that the rotes of it were all we needed to find our spirit? Small wonder that so many of our youth abandoned religion entirely, and even the loyal believers were searching more and more for answers they weren't getting from the pulpit.

Again, it seemed to be structural in our society. Exactly as we had separated the parts of our political-economic system, hadn't we also compartmentalized soul? We'd cut it out of ourselves, left it "for Sunday mornings in church." Thus, we'd rendered the miracle of our spirit as totally irrelevant as a guide for action or moral force in our lives. Ronald Reagan was a believer, but he knew instinctively: soul just didn't sell.

We seemed to have done soul in by doing religion, depersonalizing, bureaucratizing our churches until often they were little more than chummy Rotaries with a Cross. For too long, preachers of all stripes, influenced by the parts-thinking of our culture, had seen us primarily as "objects" whose main function was to pray, obey and pay---hitting us with sticks of sin and "don't's," rather than inspiring us with the do's and be's of knowing and loving ourselves as we are, where we are.

So it's natural that few of us, politicians, religious or just plain civilians can no longer understand that the being of soul, our spirit, is something far beyond politics, religion or business as usual. Because religion is only one possible expression of the human spirit, we tend to lose sight of the fact that its ultimate expression---our meaning on earth---is our search for truth.

It's learning to be me---us--- exactly who we are, in a world that is constantly trying to make us into somebody else. It is deriving our sense of worth from being our unique individuals, living for a meaning that is greater and beyond us, and therefore essential to the unfolding of all life.

Isn't it just common sense? Nobody can prove or disprove that a "God" or any kind of God figure exists, yet even the most ardent non-believer would probably admit to "feeling" some kind of life force, some greater power beyond us, whether it's nature, fate or whatever we choose to call it. If we truly believe that such a power "god" loves us---chances are "he/it" does because *something* gave us life---then can't we believe that the power loves us more for our failures than our successes. What counts is our trying. As the only one made like us, our constant trying, and failing, is our participation in the sacred of all life. Our uniqueness, our daring to be who we are in this struggle, furthers the upward progress of humanity. Each of us are irreplaceable droplets into the lake that feeds the river that feeds the sea.

If we believed that, we could rest in loving ourselves just for the truth of being ourselves and wouldn't need the confidence, stroking or reassurance of any man or any system.

Obviously, to survive, we have to earn our daily bread. But

the wisdom of the ages cautions us that we cannot live by bread alone. We have to DO, but we also have to BE. The creative tension between these two poles of ourselves is the productive electricity of our national soul.

To put our being back into our doing means that we have to go beyond ourselves. Beyond our narrow self-interests. We have to begin living for our greater or cosmic meaning.

The world we're entering now is pointing in the same direction. Globally, spirit has been awakened. The freedom cries, the revolution and chaos in many nations are the longing of other humans to live in dignity, hope and the opportunity to obtain their long-denied fair share of the essentials of life.

In the nuclear shadow, the miracle of the jet plane and instant communication, it's no longer Us versus Them. We've all become Us now.

In the central Pacific, Micronesian fishermen still paddle their traditional log canoes. Their faces and bodies are tattooed. They believe in Shark Men, Navigator Men and the ancient lore of Sea Life. Yet the day I feasted on clam with them on a palm-fringed atoll thousands of miles from anywhere, one of the little brown kids was proudly wearing a Minnesota Vikings T-shirt. How did it get there? Did he have any idea what it was?

Probably not, and it didn't matter anyway. Telecommunication and commerce crosses all boundaries. The glaring eye of TV lights the few hiding places or dark backwaters that are left. The realization has come that we all share the same human fears and the same longings to rise beyond them. All life on the planet is a single eco-system, so delicately intertwined that no species on it, including the human, can ever go it alone again. The life force, the consciousness activating this new one world, *will* prevail---with or without the United States.

The life force---humanity's survival mechanism---won't allow us to stand still. It never has before, with any society. We either change to meet the demands of our new age, or we go into the dustbin of history like so many great cultures before us. That's why the giving up of our old competitive-wantingness-war thinking has such importance. We're going to have to re-tool ourselves emotionally, intellectually, psychically and spiritually to be able to cope with the new world we're entering.

It seems to me that to activate the spirit in our own individual lives---literally jump-start our souls---we have to begin by understanding why cultures long before us have had a way of imploding and melting down. As Alexander Pope wrote about the Roman Empire: "They had no poets and they died."

No culture wants to die. God knows, we don't. But survival is a collective thing, and the thinking and actions of every one of us are like tiny trim tabs, their cumulative effect steering the leviathan of life onto uncharted shoals, or in the unison of revised thought and actions, sailing it on to a horizon bright with promise.

We live in a split-brained world. Are we put here to be, or to do, or to become whole by being/doing both? Be was the Yin of the ancient Chinese, the feminine. Do was the Yang, the masculine. The curvaceous black and white symbol of it is an equal blending of the two.

But the ancient Greeks suppressed yin, the feminine, and enthroned yang with logic and male patriarchy. The priests of the Dark Ages went even further, punishing the sinful daughters of Eve. The Crusaders sought a visionary chalice, the Holy Grail, a feminine symbol, while at the same time locking their women into chastity belts. The Renaissance managed to put men and women back into cultural equilibrium; art and progress flowered, and with it discovery. Out of this came the wholesale conquest of the New World, "a huge green Virgin to rape" in the words of philosopher, Katya Walter. Again, there was a counter-reaction. Puritainism spawned preachers and witch-burners, followed by the masculine yang of Manifest Destiny with its suppression or extermination of the dark, different yin ones, native Americans and black slaves. Almost a moment later in world time, the Industrial and High Tech revolutions took place, the supreme accomplishment of masculine yang, creating great achievements at the cost of massive bereavements, poisoning the Earth Mother and threatening the existence of all species, and even the planet itself.

"Western culture," writes Walter, "fears that huge dark power hiding deep in our cracks. It backs off from yin, the feminine, shouting, 'No! You're too witchy, irrational, entrancing. Your lure is too dangerous. I must not surrender!' So of course the culture succumbs to its repressed part. Into drugs, drink, crime, violence, dazed cults."

All these past struggles of humanity to balance its yin and yang forces and become whole have great relevance to Americans, searching to put spirit into their lives today. In the great database that consciousness is, our bodies know instinctively what has worked in human behavior and what has not worked. We've been up all the dead end roads, but in our present moment of change, a new map seems to be emerging out of the ashes of the old.

We are coming to the realization that we are not individual parts. We are not objects to be stamped out on the production line of our society. Our minds and bodies are not separate identities. They are one, and you can't treat one without treating the other. The same holds true for our politics, our economy, our Main Streets, our media, matrimony and mall. One die, all die. Psychology, philosophy, theology---science, sport and the Dow Jones---they all hit us where we live, and they cannot be compartmentalized into individual fiefdoms or multiple dualities. Every thought and action we have has been irrevocably bundled by consciousness into the one that is Us, that is our All. It is our common American soul.

Neither we nor our systems can ever go it alone again. We are all in the same leaky boat together. Our interconnectedness is our unity in diversity. It is our strength that our spirit is calling us to. Only by recognizing it and beginning to live it will we be able to put our divisive, dismantled and despairing Humpty Dumpty back together again.

In my own search for spirit, I had to ask myself: How did we get to that night of lostness with Ronnie Reagan, and even more national and personal dismay in the years since? Could it have been that the blowtorch of history was at work here, causing the meltdown of our American soul, and mine right along with it?

In the last century and a half, massive, de-stabilizing sea changes have swept across America. We weren't even born when some of them happened. We, like our ancestors, were corks tossing on the stormy seas of our heritage. Our common reaction to these great watersheds created our national psyche. Their effect upon us slowly eroded our spirit.

But in the era we're now entering---with consciousness rising at galactic speed and so many of us searching for truth---the hope is that we'll go beyond where we've been or dreamed we could ever go.

Somewhere in the distance between what we were and what we can become lies your spirit and mine, waiting for us to find it again.

8.

In the two and a half centuries from our first settlement on the Eastern seaboard up through World War I, we were shaped mainly by our immigrant heritage and the golden dream of Manifest Destiny. All of us except Native Americans had come here from somewhere else. Everyone was an invader. We had a clean slate to write on, millions of square miles of opportunity, ours for the taking.

But we also had a spirit in us, a sense of soul. The immigrants believed that each of them counted, that they had a unique meaning in the taming of this new world. Many of our Founding Fathers were not religious men, or at best they had a morality consistent with the mindset of their era. Conquest and oppression had been the handmaidens of history. They saw nothing wrong with holding slaves or refusing rights to Native Americans, "lesser" races and women. They were basically an elite clinging to the economic power they'd rapaciously plundered from the wilderness.

Yet, for all their acquisitiveness, the immigrants were believers in the spirit. The Declaration of Independence was a rocket lighting a new sky of consciousness. Humanity had never been up here before. The concept that all men were created equal was so radical and revolutionary that it stunned the world. The immigrants had shattered forever the old paradigm, and in awe at their discovery, they filled their state documents with words like "Nature's God," "Divine Providence. "In God We Trust." They looked to a Greater Power to show them their bearings and find their way. The immigrants knew who they were and blessed their lucky stars that had led them to find such a bounteous new world. From this knowledge, they derived a rock-solid courage and an almost fanatic devotion to the America they were building. It was their dream, this hard-won freedom, and it gave them a rugged frontier independence. As one European observer noted: "These Americans pass their lives without any regard to the smiles or frowns of the men in power."

The immigrants' greatest asset seemed to be their simplicity. They had come from nothing, and even when their dream showered abundance on them, they rarely forgot their rude beginnings. They accepted and welcomed their blessings, but were wary about losing their independence and becoming owned by the possession of things.

When I was a boy, I was privileged to know my immigrant grandfather, Will, and his sister Nora. In the tradition of the Irish clan sticking together, Will and Nora lived with us in our cavernous apartment on Sheridan Road on Chicago's lake shore. Only years later, when Teddy and I had three sons of our own did we return to Will's humble birthplace. On a lonely moor in County Mayo, Ireland, stands a tiny, cobbled house, whitewashed walls and a roof of thatch. The old woman who was living there at the time swept the dirt floor with a broom and invited us in for tea. "Ah, yes," she said, her eyes clouding, "this was Carney's Field. But they've all gone out long ago. God keep them."

He did.

Eleven years old, Will came to Chicago in 1866, the year after our Civil War ended. His mother and father, still in Ireland, had sent him out to make his way on what was called "The Other Side." He went to work on the Chicago docks as a tally boy, marking lumber for $4 a week. Mayo is the poorest county in Ireland, and I doubt if Will could have had much education there. When the great fire struck Chicago in 1871, Will, Nora and the younger brothers and sisters who had now joined them fled to the lakefront. They heaped what few possessions they had into a skiff and Will rowed them out to safety.

After the fire, Chicago needed rebuilding. Will traveled north into the timber of Wisconsin and Upper Michigan. He began to cut the trees and later to dig the coal that his new land required. Though he started out penniless, as Mother used to say, "He never met a stranger." He was truly amiable, not an ounce of guile in him, and most of all, a gentleness of spirit.

He was a man of peace. He never seemed to compete or fight anyone. Somehow, he managed to put together the funds or the trust to finance other pioneer lumbermen of his day, such as the Hines company in Chicago and Oregon and the Weyerhausers in the Pacific Northwest.

When telephones came in, Will saw the need to find tall timber for the poles. He sent one of his brothers, Bryan, to Spokane, Washington to start a pole company. A short time later when Bryan died, Will brought over a distant cousin from Ireland and gave him the company. Today, it's the largest of its kind in the nation. Neither Will nor our family ever received a penny out of it, nor did he expect it.

It's strange how the karma of his generosity still echoes in my own life. In the 1970's, when I was buying cattle for a ranch we had in Arizona, the owner turned out to be a man I'd never heard of, and was astonished when he knew my name well. Good reason. Early in this century, the man had been a telegrapher at Carneyville, a coal mine Will had established along the Tongue River in Wyoming. When the telegrapher contracted tuberculosis and could no longer work, Will gave him $10,000, a large sum at the time, and sent him off to recuperate in the dry air of California's Imperial Valley. The once-telegrapher not only began again but became one of the largest produce growers and ranchers in the valley, a millionaire because a man he barely knew, Will Carney, gave him his start.

Long after Will had arrived in Chicago as an immigrant boy, he was approached by another Irishman who claimed to have come over with him on the same boat. Nearly fifty years had passed. Will couldn't remember the fellow, but he said he was down on his luck and needed help. By that time, Will owned several properties in Chicago, one of them being an empty store building on the south side. His Irish compatriot begged Will to lease him the building which he'd operate as some kind of store. Will thought about it, and finally said, No, he wouldn't rent it to him, he'd give him the building. The man was overwhelmed and ashamed to accept such a gift. All he had in the world, he told Will, was several thousand acres of worthless, cut-over timber land he'd homesteaded across the lake from Chicago in Michigan. He insisted that he trade Will the land for the store. Reluctantly, Will finally accepted, and paid a few dollars in taxes every year.

When I was leaving for Navy flight training in early 1942, my father, Will's son Roy, took me across Lake Michigan on a ferry boat. We stood together out on the worthless land. Oil had been discovered on it. The rigs were already there and pumping. Not a big field, but one that repaid Will's generosity many times over for many years.

By the end of the first World War, Will had pioneered towns with his name on them in four states. He employed thousands of people, mostly immigrants like himself. He endowed hospitals and churches, and set up his brothers, sisters and their families into businesses of their own. He supported maiden aunts like Nora and other sisters, as well as his mothers' sisters.

Shortly after my mother, Marie and my father, Roy, were married, Mother as a new bride, hoping to please Will, gave him some elegant, imported shirts for Christmas. "No, no, dear," he told her gently, "they're not for me. Please take them back."

Though he was a mini-conglomerate of his day, he wore off the rack suits and worked in a cubbyhole office, meticulously recording in a tiny notebook every penny he spent---"cigars, 18 cents, taxi fare, 24 cents"---but never once wrote down how much he'd given away.

The trappings of power and privilege meant nothing to him. When his ailing wife, my grandmother, demanded that he care for her---she was mourning the death of her only other son, my namesake, Otis---Will shut his office door, turned his back on his career and took her traveling for months at a time. At his death, many businesses in Chicago and other cities he'd touched closed their doors for an hour in his memory.

Will's spirit was an inspiration to me. His natural instinct was to live in wholeness, combining the do of hard work, love of family and concern for his workers, with the be of knowing how to detach and let go of the world. When I was a kid sitting on his knee at breakfast and swiping his bacon, he'd say softly, "Moderation in all things, lad." With him, it was smoking his occassional cigar, having a whiskey or a game of golf out in the green with his friends. Many days, he'd take me by the hand and we'd stroll in silence along the lake shore, watching the sea gulls and the distant bobbing sailboats. He didn't seem to have anything to get or anyplace to be. He was already there.

The immigrant dream of people like Will and Nora was not to last very long. The magnificent isolation we'd known in wilderness America was thundered away by the storms of war in the Old World. Cavalrymen of the frontier, trained in fighting Indians, were soon leading American soldiers across the bloody battlegrounds of France. Black Jack Pershing, who'd been a lieutenant at Wounded Knee, South Dakota in the final massacre of Plains Indians, now found himself commanding the engines of the first modern war: trucks, tanks, poison gas and aircraft.

I often think of the incredible change that my father Roy saw. As a boy he'd sit by the woodstove in the mine store at Carneyville, Wyoming, and listen in fascination to tales of blanketed Sioux. Only a few years earlier, these men had fought Custer at the Little Bighorn and later his 7th Cavalry at the tragedy of Wounded Knee. What a leap it must have been for my father to remember this, when, by his own mid-twenties, he'd be learning to fly the cranky Curtiss Jenny of World War I. The contraptions of flight were so new that the Army didn't know how to classify, and finally dumped them into what they called Aviation Section Signal Corps. The only signal those planes would give would be nearly a century of dog fighting, dive bombing, fire bombing and the final mushroom cloud of the atom. From the painted braves of Custer's Massacre, my father lived to see men on the moon.

A mind-boggling, wrenching transition, but history gave us no choice. In the wiles of European statecraft and the red ink of international finance---money our banks had loaned to the Allies---we found ourselves swept back to the world the immigrants had left behind. Our leaders told us that the U.S. could never again go it alone, despite our longing for our cherished isolation.

We buried much of our immigrant dream in France. When our fathers came home, they rejoiced in the Boom, until, less than a decade later, and not knowing why, they had to begin mourning it in the Bust. And fearing for the future.

Wall Street crashed, and so did world economies. The

capitalistic free enterprise system so enshrined by the immigrants had failed to create the jobs or deliver the goods and the good life to enough of us. Now, the heirs of the immigrants, my father's generation, were cast adrift on the gray angry sea of Depression. The immigrants had not been blinded by material possessions. But it was a different story with us, the inheritors. We'd fallen in love with our things. We'd felt that abundance was owed to us. We cherished respectability and acceptance into tight-fisted Yankee society.

Thus, when the Depression threatened to sweep it all away, we had no choice but to clutch our things more desperately, lashing ourselves harder and harder to protect what we had. So often during the Depression, I remember my father coming home late from the office and sitting at the dinner table, chin in his hand and his face taut. Day after day he was having to bite the bullet, being the hard guy to relatives Will had endowed, closing the coal mines and piece-mealing off the empire Will had built. He used to tell me, "Never put off bad news. Get at it first thing in the morning. It won't go away."

The warning was implicit: get out there and fight, because if you don't, you're going to lose what's been given to you. It's human nature to be competitive, and no single trigger touches off an increase of it. But the Depression girded us with a special sort of fear. We felt as if we were in a war that swirled across the dark streets of Chicago. In working class neighborhoods where I wasn't supposed to go, I'd see angry men, warming themselves beside flame lit barrels, and trying to sell me an apple. When I'd refuse in fright, they'd say, "Fuck you, richie."

From our school games to our corporate boardrooms, we were honed on the Performance Ethic. Money-getting and money-keeping was to be our goal and meaning in life. We were judged on what we do, what we earn, not on what we were as human beings. Our embattled creed had shifted from Christ to Calvin: if it didn't hurt, it wasn't good for you. And lest we forget, we were raised on horror stories: "Three generations, shirtsleeves to shirtsleeves." "The squeaky wheel gets the grease." Up and at it. Men fight. Men win!

In 1937, psychologist Karen Horney identified the forces

that were robbing our spirit: "Aggressiveness grown so pronounced that it could no longer be reconciled with Christian brotherhood; desire for material goods so vigorously stimulated that it can never be satisfied; expectations of untrammeled freedom soaring so high that they cannot be squared with the multitudes of restrictions and responsibilities that confine us all."

Relentlessly, we began to classify ourselves according to what achievements we'd made in competition with our peers. We learned to objectify each other not as fellow humans but rivals in our fight through the jungle of the industrial world. In our schools and colleges, shadowed by the Depression, we learned that sports' letters, attractiveness, popularity and leadership were the attributes deemed essential for success. We wanted to be seen as comers so that we could separate ourselves from the pack and be guaranteed our share of the economic pie.

When I was at Princeton in 1941, one of my classmates was so desperate to "make" our eating club, he broke down before us and wept. He was a legacy of old immigrant wealth. Getting into our particular exclusive club was the last chance he felt he had to prove his social worth and value as a human being. But as one of our In-group put it, "Oh, don't take that clod. What's he ever *done*? He's a first-rate second-rate guy." And so, rejected, he sobbed away, a loser in a winner's world.

The Competitor Ethic, branded on us in the Depression, left enduring scars.

Years later, when I decided to leave what my mother called "legitimate" business---it was advertising at the time---and become a free-lance writer, working at home, a neighbor lady was shocked. "Why," she asked, "aren't you on the Train, commuting to the city?"

I mumbled something about my writing dream, but the woman couldn't process it. Nobody we knew *wrote*. Sympathetically, she said, "This flu that's going around is a terrible bug. You just rest at home a few days, you'll get over it."

I never did. Decades later, when Teddy and I decided to raise our kids out on a cattle ranch, one of their godmothers said in alarm: "It may be fine for a summer vacation, but it's so risky. Suppose they get to *like* the life?"

To the competitors, liking, loving your living, trying to get at the truth of yourself instead of hurting in acceptable work and denying your spirit---no, that was the ultimate cop-out. The falling between the cracks: the societal death sentence.

And then, too soon, the deaths became real. They would be our own.

World War II hurled an even greater challenge at our competitive creed. For our very survival now, we had to learn to suppress the peaceful instincts of our spirits and let our killer reflexes take over. The only way we could destroy our enemies was to whip up massive hatred against them.

From the objectifying we'd practiced in our social and business lives, and the powers of propaganda we'd developed to sell each other our things, it was only a short step to turning our enemy into a fiend, a sub-human. The last night before I went off to war, my parents had a goodbye party for me. One of my father's friends, a man I'd revered---football hero, decorated in World War I, business leader, all the things that seemed to matter---boozily, he grabbed me and with a wincing punch on my arm, chortled: "Get one for me, boy!"

One? One what? A sports letter, a good job after the war? No, one was an object to hang on our wall. A Jap or a Kraut.

One night in Honolulu, June, 1944, a pretty Japanese nurse I'd been seeing sneaked me into her room in the civilian hospital where she worked. We were giggling, thinking we'd put one over on the race and caste system.

Not for long. The door banged open, the head nurse, a towering American amazon thrust in on us. She snatched up my khaki cap and screamed: "You! A Marine lieutenant! How could you *be* with that Jap!"

Four days later on Guam's Orote Point, I be'd with them all right, walking over their bodies, hunks of flesh blown apart in the insane banzai charge they'd made just hours before we landed. Severed arms still clinging to samurai swords. Cut off heads, grimacing goblins in the mud, and flies eating their eyes.

We parked our plane beside a concrete bunker that had been an enemy machine gun position. Inside it were 28 blackened lumps. The attacking Marines had torched them with a flamethrower. For the next two weeks, we lived with the sweet, sickening smell of human flesh. Mel, our crewchief, cried out, "Can't somebody bury those poor bastards!" But nobody ever did. No time for it in a war.

They were just Japs. "Ones."

In almost two years of flying in the Pacific, from Guadalcanal to Okinawa, my own objectifying of the enemy had so benumbed me that when we blew off our two atomic bombs, I had no feeling whatsoever for the burned ash streaks on the Japanese earth. I just thanked God that it was them, not us, and now we could rush home and enjoy the peace we'd won.

What none of us could foresee was that peace would never happen. The immigrant dream was long gone down. Those of us in the two world war generations now had to become defenders of our way of life.

Good reason, we thought. Risen out of the war rubble of 1945 emerged our latest enemy, the Soviet Union and its chilling battle cry of world communism.This patently evil system threatened to take away our things. It was imperative that we defend democratic free enterprise, by war if necessary, just as the Russians were ordered to defend socialist peace, also by war. Double-speak. Words no longer meant what they once had.

From 1945 onward, we were asked to live the lie of the warfare state. For the first time in our history, we found ourselves literally scared to death. The atomic weapons we'd loosed on humanity were now poised to be used against us. We and the Russians alike were trapped in a mutual death dance of pathologic horror, lest either side be wiped out by another Pearl Harbor surprise attack.

In our terrible fear, irresistibly manipulated by what Gore Vidal calls "our managers," a great change came over America. No longer were we the "strong loud voices unafraid," or the self-reliant immigrants who could "pass their lives without any regard to the smiles or frowns of the men in power."

Now instead, we cringed before our leaders. Only they could save us from technological forces gone mad. Up until at least the Depression, we had always regarded government as the servant of the people. The bureaucrats worked for us. But now, we abdicated our independence. Eagerly, we handed over our freedom to a government that would protect us from annihilation.

And the whole shoddy business was a fraud.

Two years after the war ended, I was working as a fledgling reporter on the Minneapolis _Star_. My desk-mate, an old news veteran, thrust me a teletype just off the wire from Washington. It was labeled euphemistically "Department of Defense," the new goliath that had swallowed our previously separate services. Perhaps our old War Department moniker connoted too much naked aggression for the spin-doctors who were now imaging us as noble defenders.

"Russian bomber sighted over Alaska," my desk-mate said bitterly. "Wake up, kid, don't you get it?"

"Get what?"

"They've got a fight over military appropriations coming up in Congress this week. So they've got to scare the dummies into giving them more dough. Next week, count on it, they'll probably surface a Russian sub off of California."

I thought: You cynical bastard, you sit out four years of war behind your desk and now you're the expert. "Aw come on," I said, "our government doesn't work that way."

We had to learn that it did, from then on. Dwight Eisenhower knew it when in his final speech as President, he warned us about the incredible power of the military-industrial complex, which was beginning to take over our lives. We were launching the Cold War to bring our "freedom" (e.g. a free market to sell our goods in) to peoples whom we regarded as backward, 3rd world, and so we partitioned humanity into Us versus Them.

Of course the Soviet Union was dangerous. They had nuclear weapons and immense armed forces. But they had also lost an estimated 22 million of their people in World War II. Despite their diabolical threats, they were a wasted, basically primitive nation, leading from bluff more than strength. They dreaded the horror of another war, and lived in fear that we would wreak one upon them. Justifiably so, because our containment policy had encircled them in a ring of steel.

But the hollowness of the Soviet threat was downplayed by our leaders. We bought into the Cold War myth because it created jobs, a horn of plenty pumping out our Good Life, and thus we accepted the crushing debt and reduced freedoms of a warfare state, scarring our land with missile sites, and spreading its tentacles to 110 military bases world-wide. We became the greatest colonial power ever saddled on the back of mankind. At home, defense contracts were crafted to dole out employment to every congressional district. Our leaders had convinced us that defending our way of life was more important than all life. And the flip side of the patriotism song had an uglier tone, a truth that was carefully never mentioned. Our system of democracy/free enterprise/capitalism only seemed able to work if we kept fueling it by building the killing machines of war.

By the end of our defending, we and the Enemy, including the "clients' we'd both armed, had managed between us to kill more human beings that had died in both World War I and World War II combined. Together, we had created the bloodiest century in human history.

Give up war? Go beyond ourselves to the victory of surrender? No, it will never be ours until we let our spirit become again the controlling force of our lives. Put it back into us by changing the way we as individuals and nation think and act.

Stop the doomsday pendulum. How many wars do we need to teach us that violence always begets violence?

The soul of a nation is a fragile thing. It melts away perilously fast. Our spirit *knows* the difference between truth and lies. Just as the women's bodies reacted by reflex to "wanting what you have"---my throw-away line in the California speech---so do our individual and national bodies react to cultural lies being foisted off on us day and night. We know instinctively they're not true. We protest them. We mourn, grieve, make ourselves sick in anger.

Because what can we do? We're dazed, separated, alienated---cut off objects. Parts of a system that no longer hears us.

How do we bring truth into our lives and stop swallowing this guff?

We have to spike the lies and unmask the demons we've been sold. We bought into them because we were acting out of fear or desire. These understandable human failings have always been ripe for manipulation. But once we face the denial we've been living in and forgive ourselves for it, our leap to courage will take us beyond myth and into the hope of truth.

9.

To open yourself up to the spirit requires a change of mindset.

It's the chicken or the egg riddle. Which comes first? Does spirit come knocking at your door and cause you to change? Or does your change cause spirit to enter your life?

You don't go looking for it. You usually don't even know when your change began. All you really glimpse are flash moments of peak experiences that make your road, for that instant at least, a little more clear.

In 1973, the old world I'd known was ending.

Forty-two years after my boyhood night of cringing in our apartment, waiting for the Japs to come, I was on a jet, thundering west across the Pacific from Honolulu to Guam. It was an odd way to begin a holiday, with a lump in my throat, and I suspected it wouldn't be the last time I'd feel it. In the darkening cabin of the 707, Teddy had fallen asleep beside me. The other passengers seemed ghostlike, their faces silvered in the flickering light of the movie screen. So nobody was going to notice a middle-aged fellow, sipping a bourbon and occasionally dabbing at his eyes as he stared down at the empty sea.

Looking for what? I wondered. The three decades that had fled past in the clouds, the memories of that time when we were all out here in this Pacific, young, bursting with bravado and ideals. The war that would remove evil from the world. We'd prayed that it wouldn't end before we could get into it. And of course, it didn't end. We'd had no peace. Only the names of our enemies had changed, and it was they who had snatched our victory from us and given us decades of defeat. Korea, Cuba, Vietnam, we were losing, counting the bodies of our sons and wondering why we couldn't win anymore.

It was this sense of frustration that was leading me back to the islands. I felt drawn by some strange, psychic force. Something had to be resolved here, my instinct was saying.

Could there be something else left out in this Pacific, some barnacled iron relic that might be a memory of courage? As if in looking at the old, hard-won places again, I might be able to say: well, at least, we did that. We won, here.

I felt a keen loneliness now. On St. Patrick's Day that year, my father, Roy, had died. Though he'd been in failing health for some time, his death was the ending of an era. I'd miss him greatly. In this dark night over the Pacific, I remembered sadly all the islands where I'd stood in the rain at mail call. Invariably, there'd be a letter from Roy that said without saying: he was with me wherever I was.

The captains and kings had departed. Teddy's young brother, Bill, was a Marine rifleman slogging through some rice paddy on his second tour in Vietnam. He said he'd joined the Corps because of my stories. But the voice that had told them was far less certain now. After the Goldwater debacle of 1964, I wrote no more politics, either in film or novel. I had a feeling that all the words in the world couldn't change the direction of the nation. Locked in our no-win war, we seemed to be playing out a death wish. What was dying, I realized, were the values I deeply believed in. God was a myth, patriotism a dirty word, scrawled in the graffiti of the Sixties Revolution.

Like the plaintive song of the hippie rebels: "Where have all the flowers gone?" I neither knew, nor had much hope of ever seeing them again.

From the first moment we landed on Guam, it struck me like the stifling heat and the blaze of sun. Nothing I had known was here anymore. A stranger had seen it, not me. Where I'd remembered adventure and horror, Guam was now traffic-jammed, smoggy Americanized banality, as romantic as north San Diego, another arsenal city that appeared to have spawned it.

So surrender first the dream that the war we'd fought here in our youth had meant something. Our crusade that would change the world, and those who had died in this last of all wars had not died in vain. Forlorn, steaming islands, I wanted only to weep at the non-meaning of it all.

Oblivion. Dead flesh, feeding the living coral.

On Guam's Orote Point, where I had stepped over hunks of

Japanese bodies, blown apart in their insane banzai charge, now a garrison U.S. Navy had built a supermarket and paved the slaughter site with ball diamonds, tennis courts and tract houses. As for the bomb-pocked airstrip where we'd lived for uncounted days in our plane, beside the concrete bunker reeking with incinerated Japanese bodies---only a grassy knoll remained. Orote had disappeared. Beyond in the harbor, skeletons clawed at the sky: groaning cranes and drydocks that were readying our fleet to attack our present enemies in Vietnam. On the horizon, overlooking the bloody invasion beaches rose clusters of gleaming white hotels. "American?" I asked my cab driver. He shook his head. "They're all either owned or operated by Japs. It's their favorite honeymoon resort. They come here by the thousands."

So what had we won in our suffering and sacrifice? Instead of ridding ourselves of the Japanese "demons," we'd married them. And when I finally fled from Guam and reached the isolated beaches of Pelelieu, the futility of our battle there was even more heart-rending.

The island that I had left as a hideous wasteland, blackened by napalm firestorms, was now a green jungled mound, scars healed and lofty barringtonia trees forming a rain-forest canopy over the grisly tombs of Bloody Nose Ridge.

Wild pigeons fluttered out of the abbatoir of Japanese caves. Wild bantam chickens pecked through dark tunnels where enemy handgrenades lay in neat rows, waiting to be hurled. In the sepulchral gloom lay tins of Japanese fish, helmets, American bayonets and first aid kits. Left where they had fallen thirty years before. Untouched. Forgotten.

The airfield, where the ammo dump had blown away my war novel and my heroine Teddy, was an impenetrable plain of tall grass. With his bare, black foot, a Palauan native scuffed at the grass until he'd exposed a streak of coral. His teeth were stained red with betel nut, and they shone in a grin. "Belonga here big bird, come fly away, long time." Fly away, Teddy Fly.

Twenty-two thousand humans were wounded or died on Pelelieu, more than a third of them Americans. Yet the Palauan natives told me that before Teddy and I were there, only a handful of Americans had ever returned. But the Japanese had come often, going up into the caves and recovering incinerated bones that they hoped belonged to their ancestors. In ceremonial boxes, they brought them back to the Homeland for proper burial.

As for the Americans who had given their lives here, at the time we visited, there was neither a sign nor single remembrance. When I left the island and slid back across the reef in a native outboard, I had tears in my eyes. Ah, God, what had it all been for?

Rust, junk and death. I wanted to flee it and head home, but to get there, we had to make a final stop at Truk atoll. I had bad memories of the place.

For two nights, August 13-14, 1944, General Geiger had ordered us to fly from Guadalcanal up to Guam and return. To make the trip by the most direct and urgent route, we'd have to fly directly though enemy airspace, a thousand miles each way, sneaking past the dreaded Truk which was Japan's Pearl Harbor in the Pacific. We had no escort. Fighters didn't have the range to accompany us. Our only armament was two Thompson submachine guns.

The urgency, we were later told, was to bring back to Geiger crates of plans for the Pelelieu operation, less than a month away. His staff officers had been working on them during the Guam battle.

To pull it off, we'd have to hit in the darkness a 60 mile slot between two atolls, Puluwat and Lamotrek. One had an enemy fighter strip, the other a seaplane base. Should we drift too close to either one, their radar would pick us up and they'd blow us out of the sky.

Going up the first night, and using celestial navigation, we must have hit the slot. We slept all day in a wrecked building at Guam. When we awakened and prepared to take off with the plans, one of the blackest, lightning-flashed storms we'd ever seen was roaring down on Guam. We'd have to sock right into it to get home. The rain was so heavy it came through the window seals and soaked us in the cockpit. The turbulence was violent, two thousand feet a minute up, then roaring back down. We were wildly out of control. We had no stars to shoot, nothing to steer by. It was impossible to hit our slot between Puluwat and Lamotrek. When we neared their estimated position, we shut off our radios. We literally tried to whisper past. When the radioman spotted running lights paralleling us, he shouted: "Jap!" It must have been. We think a Betty bomber, heavily armed and possibly looking for us in the wildness of the storm.

The only thing we could do was to plunge into massive, fisting thunderheads and lose ourselves. We accomplished it, but unfortunately, we also lost our destination airstrip on tiny Emirau Island. After hours of wandering lost, we finally begged them in plain language, not code: if they heard us, turn a searchlight up at the sky. After what seemed more hours of bad sky-road, we finally saw its light rubbing the dark clouds. We roared down and landed with our gas gauge needles ticking on empty.

Why was it that now, nearly 30 years later, I'd be taking shelter from a storm on the Truk beach and giving a light to a soaked Trukese fisherman? On the wet brown skin of his back, I noticed ugly scars. "Japan time," he said. They had bayonetted him and forced him to work for them building airfields. He sucked at the cigarette he'd rolled and his coffee eyes studied me. "You know Japan time? You come here like other 'Merican guys, break oil tanks, plenty smoke, bomb going off?"

I said no, that was the big carrier strike in '44, but a few months later, I did fly near here for a couple of nights, through Puluwat and Lamotrek.

He howled. "Lamotrek!" He clasped my hand, then threw his arms around me. "I raised on Lamotrek! Home island. Maybe I there them nights! Look up in sky, see you!"

With the rain drumming the thatch roof, we talked long of the wartime days until finally he gripped both of my hands. "Yah, we same, you know us here, we friends. Hey, 'Merican guy, I got place you gonna see. Beautiful. Best we got. Tomorrow, I take you in my fishing boat. What you think? We go Paradise Island!"

Oh, come on, I thought. Was this a tourist scam or something he was making up?

But Paradise existed and we went to it the next day. Max, the fisherman, his boat boy David, Teddy and me. And at the last minute, we had a passenger from Tokyo. Akio was his name, a sweet, earnest young employe of the Japanese Tourist Bureau. Down here to explore tourist facilities in the area, he was prototype Japanese, white shorts and shirt, knee socks and camera around his neck. He kept thanking us effusively for including him on our trip.

But as we roared across Truk lagoon, the largest in the world, I think Akio began to wonder why he'd come. Max was running the tiller of his outboard with his bare foot, and even over the noise of his Johnson 50 horse, he was barking angry Japanese at Akio. They were re-fighting their war now, Max having been a much abused prisoner. Akio would turn away, his face so tight with humiliation that Teddy and I felt embarrassed to watch. But then, like an island storm, it swept on past. Max scrambled up to the bow and flung out his arm. "There, 'Merican guy! Paradise!"

It was spectacular, a fragment of island no more than a reef, white sand beaches shaded with palms. Inland, beyond a thicket of heavy mangroves, I could make out the seaward side, naked battlements of coral, pounded by the open Pacific and thundering misty spume hundreds of feet into the air. The roar was constant and awesome, a symphony of rainbows, seabirds arching in screaming parabolas and plunging into the shattering waves for prey.

Max slowed the boat and we glided over vermilion and ochre coral gardens. Schools of brightly colored fish drifted below us through forests of yellow lace. They didn't seem to sense our presence. They made no attempt to run away. When Teddy and I slid into the warm softness of the water and coasted through the coral gardens in the suck and hiss of our snorkels, the fish were so tame they'd stream between our legs. Some would even gup their mouths on the strange taste of our tennis shoes.

"Bad sharks here?" I asked David, our boat boy who was paddling beside us. He was grinning, wearing a mar-mar headband of green leaves. "No bad." A moment later, a dark shadow appeared in my face mask. An eight foot shark, lazily studying us and drifting on past.

The scene was so fierce and primeaval, so remote from any "civilized" world that I seemed to lose consciousness of time and my place within it. Here, I was part of the eternal struggle of the coral to replenish itself. I was the crash and suck and refueling of the waves, my energy somehow tied to all of it. The trembling reef beneath my feet was connected in its bedrock to the ancient burned-out volcanoes that had formed the atolls of Puluwat and Lamotrek. My nights of fear above those islands---how insignificant they'd been against nature's flaming struggles through her eons of time. That was the real and only war, the nobility of her life force, pulsing in every particle of living matter, coding into them the ultimate meaning that life would prevail.

Behind me I heard a human cry, and reluctantly I turned away from the thundering reef. Akio was dog-paddling toward me, spluttering apologies. I'd loaned him my spin-fishing rod, and now he'd managed to lose my only lure. He was determined to send me a dozen lures from Japan, please?

I smiled and told him to forget it. We hadn't really come here to fish. But as we paddled on together into a hidden bay, I spotted a silver metal fin, protruding from the shallow water. I gulped a deep breath and dove, then blew out a gasp of astonishment when I saw it. Resting on the soft sand bottom was a Zero fighter, not a mark of rust on it or a scar. It appeared to have landed here moments before. I clung to the canopy of the open cockpit, fully expecting to see a skeleton within. But there was only emptiness and the red needle of the airspeed indicator ticking in tiny bubbles.

Akio clung to the tail section as I made repeated dives. In the sand I found a fragment of the Zero's wing flap, which seemed to be the only damage when the pilot crash-landed. As I carried the relic back to shore, my mind was spinning. Who was in that plane? Had he been some eager, untried youth, fighting our fleet in the carrier strike? Did he parachute out? Or could it have been possible that he, too, had been ordered to fly that night of August 14, sent up into the storm to chase an American bogey that had somehow slipped away between Puluwat and Lamotrek?

Lost in the enigma of it, I sat in the warm sand and studied the fragment of flap. Akio knelt beside me. I showed him splinters of wood, laminated between the Zero's outer skin. I was amazed that they'd used wood. Akio nodded. Yes, bamboo. That's all Japan had left by the end of the war.

His voice had tightened, his eyelids squeezed shut. In dignity, he was weeping. At first I pretended not to notice, but then he touched my arm gently and said, "It is Japan's fault, all this here. So much destruction, so much horror we caused. I knew nothing about it. I wasn't born then. But my father had to go. He fought…" He shook his head and tears ran down his cheeks. "What we did, I am so sorry…"

When I answered, my throat was tight. "It's nobody's fault," I said. "Put it behind us. It's done now."

Then, in a moment, the awkwardness was gone. From down the beach Max was shouting to us. He'd speared a giant clam and came sloshing in from the reef with a purpling, blobby object in his hand. By the time Akio and I reached him, he'd sliced the muscle from the clam and was drenching it in lime juice and soy sauce. We ate it raw, washing it down with Kirin beer, and then stretched out under the palm trees.

Teddy lay sunburned in the sand and looked as lithe as she had at 21. Even the sea tousle of my hair I could consider as resembling salt, not grey. Whatever our delusions, we felt a youth and liberation, unfettered by wrist watches and the baggage of our cares. Trukese, Japanese, American, we seemed joined into the life force, our strangeness to each other and our enmities fading away.

As if to heighten the unreality, we began hearing new sounds from out on the reef. Distant dots moved toward us across the coral flats until they became native canoes. Tapping their paddles against the wooden hulls, two boatloads of Trukese fishermen glided up to our beach. Max hailed them and they spilled out, the women waddling up in their bright mumus, several of them squatting shamelessly in the shallows to complete their toilets before joining us. Max told me that these were several families of fishermen, from babes at the breast to wizened elders with blue tattoos in the wrinkles of their cheeks.

They lay with us in the shade of the mangroves, their brown limbs melting into the sand in instant relaxation.

Time and ambition seemed meaningless to them. They were children of the Stone Age, and how they could laugh! A young girl lazily draped her arm around me. That was funny. Then, she tweaked my beaky nose---that was hilarious. The others were belching, rumbling, snoring, and when they drifted back to wakefulness, their eyes caught the endless reflection of the sea. Soon, with Max translating, they began telling us tales of the great ocean voyages of the Micronesian people. They spoke of the Magic Men who were trained generation after generation to guide the canoes across thousands of miles of open sea. Riding with them, too, were the Navigator Men who could track the stars with the naked eye, watch the direction of birds and the coloration of the water to give them their bearings.

Sea life, they called it, and to preserve their lives on their journeys was the Shark Man. Trained from childhood to sing a special mantra, he could slip into the water and confront a massive shark that was threatening the canoe. Because ocean waves swamped the canoes, these Micronesians were often sitting in water with the shark's great fin only a few feet away. But armed only with his mantra chant, the Shark Man would approach the monster, gentle him until he could rub his belly. Then he'd slip a mar mar of palm leaves over the shark's head and he'd drift harmlessly away.

I glanced at Teddy. She was sitting bolt upright, half-frown, half rapture. Could we believe such a thing? No, certainly not back home in our normal lives. But Paradise Island, the sudden confronting of the past buried within us, the primeaval spirit--- was this not also home, the real one?

Then, like most moments of grace, too soon it was over. Without any predetermined signal, the Trukese left us, their laughter trailing down to their canoes, and their footprints in the sand were slowly washed away by the creeping tide.

They disappeared toward the falling sun until they were tiny specks again, floating off to probe some other reef. We, too, departed then, our bodies sunburned, our limbs soft and nerveless from hours in the sea. As we rumbled across the enormity of Truk atoll, a night of yellowish stars closed over us. Sometime in the long trip home, Akio, perhaps thinking of his own wife, said to Teddy: "Ah, madam, please tell me: what flowers do you choose for your arrangements?"

I stared at him in the darkness. You, my enemy? You the demon I was taught to hate? Where would the next one be? The boat's wake slid away behind us, bubbling silver now in the rising of the moon.

10.

Do you awaken to your spirit in a single incident, or is it on-the-job training?

Our job, back then, was filming a not-quite adult TV western. Out in the sagebrush of Wyoming, in the shadow of the Tetons, we built a false-fronted frontier town. This was make-believe. We were re-creating 1876, and bringing into the wilderness a happy little family of pioneers. The Monroes, we called them, in a series I'd created for 20th Century Fox and ABC.

Ma and Pa Monroe and their five kids had come west in a covered wagon. They were searching for a splendid mountain valley that Pa had seen during his earlier western military service. Now, if they could stumble onto it again, they'd homestead Pa's valley and turn it into their new life. Paradise found.

But the gimmick was, these kids had to go it alone. The network thought it would beef the ratings if we had orphans braving the wilderness, meaning we lose Ma and Pa in the heart-rending first episode. So, with all the fanfare of a big production, which it was, we built a raft and thrust the Monroe wagon, parents, kids, faithful dog and Iowa cow out into the icy Snake River. A stuntman and stunt woman were playing Ma and Pa. In midstream, pretending they'd tripped, they toppled into the current and to the wails of their kiddies, were swept away. They were wearing wet-suits. They knew how to do stuff like this, but for reasons known only to the movie god, they refused to sink. The camera followed two black little heads, bobbing relentlessly downstream. From the cutting room at 2oth Century Fox came a roar. Why in hell hadn't we managed to drown the buggers? Cursing, the editors had to ink out their heads frame by frame.

Only a moment later in movie time, we prepared to shoot the epic scene of the first episode. Our little orphans, wandering lost in the wilderness, now manage by Hollywood miracle to stumble onto Pa's fabled valley. The thrill of it rocketed the director to new heights. At great expense he brought in a crane that could have lifted the moon missile and elevated the camera on top of it. Looking back down on our precious kids, he shot dramatic closeups of each, dashing up the long grassy hill, breathlessly reaching the crest, and then, in squeals of joy and tears, beholding Pa's valley just below. As Brigham Young said, seeing Salt Lake for the first time, "This is the place!"

Realistically, on their own, the kids couldn't have found their way out of a McDonalds, so I'd inserted an Indian character, Jim, to pathfind them up to the historic moment. But the casting director either didn't know any real Indians or couldn't find one down at Hollywood and Vine, so instead he chose a nice, athletic white kid. There was only one problem. Hollywood Jim was Jewish from the Bronx and had never been on a horse in his life. Again, to keep the movie-ishness out of it we'd found him a true Indian pinto pony that he'd ride bareback. No way, Jose. The horse was supposed to canter but Jim couldn't sit even a slow walk. When he kept falling off and ruining takes, we finally stooped to tying a rope around the pinto that Jim could cling to as his security blanket and we covered it with an actual period Indian blanket. We finally got him cantering up to the crest like a lopsided sack of potatoes, but he made it. They all did. We had our shot, the big moment. The director was jumping in glee and everyone cheered.

Meanwhile back at the ranch, down at Fox, they looked at the footage and I got a call. "Where," said a dismal voice, "is Pa's valley?"

"How was that again?"

"Pa's Valley, goddammit! Your director got so carried away with his crane shot, sure, he got all the reactions of the kids, but WHAT the hell were they looking AT? *We have no shot of the fuckin' valley!*"

By the time this tiny error was discovered, the icy blasts of fall had swept across Wyoming. Our discovery crest of long green grass and the verdant valley beyond were now frozen yellow and dying. Panic set in. We couldn't get a shot of our actual valley until next summer, and the show was due on in ten days. In a mad scramble through film vaults and photo libraries, the editors finally located a postcard still shot of some no-name paradise valley. Nobody knew where it was and audience wouldn't care anyway. They and our happy little family just had to make-do with the make-believe of it.

But not for long. After twenty-six progressively sillier one hour episodes, our hardy pioneers were sent trooping off to their last roundup in the Neilsen rating sky. I wrote the epitaph in the final show of the series. In some desperate clutch at creativity, I invented a traveling circus that happened to be passing through the area. To give our kids a last laugh in their tears, I brought them into the fake town we'd built and let them play around in the circus. I had no idea why I'd named the town what I had. There were dozens of other pioneer words that would have rung true, instead of one that I'd almost never used. But in some occult stroke of consciousness, I'd happened to call the town Paradox.

What is the power that converts you?

Does spirit burst upon you in a single ecstatic moment of "born again?" Now you *know* The Truth!

Or is spirit, like the false-fronted town, the paradox that you and I are stuck with? Do you rush up to the crest of discovering paradise, only to find yourself lost in a cloud of unknowing? It's all mirages, trick camera angles. You get the reaction shot but you never see what you saw. What is true in one glance is not true in the next. The pioneers' search is both/and. You never reach Pa's valley because it is both there and not there.

In the mystery, there are no certainties. Only Paradox. Ghost town. Holy Ghost.

To give up your war---to let go---you have to go with the mystery.

All the spirit tells you is that you are the sum of your choices. You took this road in life instead of that road, not necessarily because you chose to do it, but because your spirit has chosen the one that preserves its life in you.

A friend asked Teddy: "When did you have your conversion moment?"

"I didn't."

"Didn't? You mean nothing happened, you had no born again experience?"

"No, not at all. It was just something that always seemed to be there. I had nothing to do with it. When I was a little girl, I used to go pray with the flowers in Mother's rose garden. I had no idea why. I had no training in saying prayers. It just felt right, and made me happier than anything I'd ever known."

The friend sighed. "I wish it were so simple. I keep waiting for my moment."

In one way or another, we're all on call waiting in the chambers of our private purgatories. We can't help it. We live in an culture that demands certitude. We want definitive answers---*now*. We expect them. We want to be told that this is right, and that is wrong, and there is no gray area between them. Give us the Fundamentals! Show us How we're supposed to live, wrap it in a box and take it home, pull up the covers, go to sleep and never think about it again.

That's that!

And yes, you can catch flashes of spirit, like a pretty girl showing leg. You can have snapshots of grace, freeze frames of peak experiences, but the movie has more reels than you'll ever have time to see. You never get to say, This is where I came in and now I can leave. It's not an all night Drive In, it's an all life Drive In, the movie you're playing is finding and losing and finding again, day by day, moment by moment---and all the popcorn you can eat.

In our hunger for certainty, it galls us when we can't pigeonhole people and find out what they stand for. Who-is-this-guy? Where-is-that-gal-coming- from? Are you one of us or not?

After I'd written a political satire called <u>Throw the Rascals Out,</u> a friend who'd read it said to my brother, "I always thought Otis was a normal guy, good Republican, conservative. Now he's coming on like a damn populist radical. Which is he?"

My brother smiled and shook his head. "Frankly, we don't know what the hell he is, or how he got that way."

The sub-text: you had to have had a born-again moment, didn't you? Something must have changed you, to drive you away from the tribe.

Again, it goes back to spirit. You are the sum of the choices spirit makes for you. I can't tie up in any neat package what led me from being a belonger to my heritage, a Goldwater conservative---"better to piss inside the tent than outside," as LBJ said. Yet for me to rocket from this so-called certitude all the way out through the back of the tent until I was standing at least to the left of Noam Chomsky---why? What my spirit had led me to was a radical no-man's land where there were no political labels and no fortresses of fear to have to keep defending. Me and my shadow, like the song. Or maybe it was like the old Irishman, Pat. Just naturalized as a U.S. citizen, a friend asked him, "Well, Pat, now that you can vote, what are you going to be? Democrat?"

"Go to hell, lad."

"Republican, then?"

"Go to hell twice."

"But Pat, you've got to vote for something."

"I do, and I will."

"What?"

"Agin' the guv'mint!"

My trouble is, I've always loved the "guv'mint.' I've served it. I've thrilled at its nobility. I still do, loving it for the country it represents. The greatest in the world, in charity, productivity, optimism, courage and ingenuity. That's why it's so lonely outside the tent. Because here, spirit seems to be howling on the night wind: you have to be who you are. Not them. Much as you admire and love them, when they and their systems crush your spirit and that of others, you have no choice but to go it alone, and to speak truth, as little of it as you can know, to their power. Because if it suppresses truth---if it's not your truth which you feel so keenly, but rather if it's injustice on any level---then you have no choice but to remove yourself from it. And in patience, and above all in non-judgemental kindness, forgive them for their humanness. They know not what they do, and neither do you most of the time. Admit it! All you can do is to speak what your heart tells you, and not care if no one ever hears.

It was a long road. I don't know where it began, only that I had a loving family, the silver spoon and freedom from any want. As the second child who, as my mother said about my grandfather, Will, "never met a stranger," I learned early on how to work the system. My gentle Irish nurse, Theresa, spoiled me rotten. I'd lie on my bed feigning incredible fatigue, and sweet Theresa would pull up my long stockings and dress me. We had an Irish cook, too, and I'd con her into making my junkets and milk toasts, separate meals for the little prince. At night, under a picture of Jesus with his lambs, Theresa would kneel me down and make me say with her:

"Angel of God, my guardian dear,

To whom his love commits me Here,

Ever this night be at my side,

To light and guard, to rule and guide."

Then we'd sing: "I went to the Animal Fair, the birds and the beasts were there." I went to sleep knowing that every day was going to be more lucious than the one just passed. My little paradise would never have an end.

But life, like baseball which I played and loved, knocks hard grounders at you. The runner is streaking for second base. Do you throw him out and then try for the double play at first? Or are you so busy planning, controlling what you do that the ball goes right through your legs and into the outfield? The crowd groans. You've blown it again.

Pretty soon, you stop hearing the crowd. The spirit voice in you is saying: be you, not them. If your culture has raised you to fight, are you a coward for not pitching in and beating the shit out of life? Okay, then, be a coward. Listen to your spirit---and dare not be smug because you happen to be hearing a different drummer than the rest do.

So there was no conversion moment, no one Eureka light flashing in my head. It was a kaleidiscope of a thousand episodes, snap shots, freeze frames of values I wanted, and others, in pain and often tears, I had to reject. They weren't me.

They weren't taking me where my spirit said I had to go.
 The cloud of unknowing. That's the paradox.
 I can't even put words to the song.
 I'm not right and you're not wrong.
 It's just trust, I think,
 That leads us to do what we must.

11.

When we were filming <u>Cinerama</u> <u>Holiday,</u> we did a sequence in a black church in Louisiana, the congregation joyously booming out the grand old spiritual "Down by the Riverside."

The second line was: "I ain't gonna study war no more, I ain't gonna study war no more…"

Soul war, they were talking about. I can only hope your journey to the battleground of enlightenment has less miles of bad road in it than the one I took. Or, I should say, the one I was dragged onto, kicking and screaming.

I can't blame Teddy. I love her for it, and envy her courage in searching so diligently for the spirit. She can listen for hours to tapes or wade through industrial-strength theology tomes that glaze my eyes over on page one. She's an intellectual, devouring ideas I simply can't swallow with my limited equipment. I tell her it's because she grew up in the South where beauty was worshipped and a pretty girl wasn't supposed to have a brain. All these years, she's been proving the good ole boys wrong.

But by the early '80's, her desire for sanctity began to include me, and as someone said when the Teletubby dolls were introduced, "Be very afraid." She was determined to get me out of my spiritual closet. Straight from Calvin: "If it didn't hurt, it wasn't good for me."

Oh-oh, I thought, what now? In the past, I'd usually send her off alone to her retreats, seminars and holy gatherings that our sons call "Catholic Camps." But this time, we were into major league soul war.

She was going to take me 10,000 miles around the world to an ashram in southern India. Our very own bed of nails.

When I protested, she reminded me of all the lousy fishing trips I'd dragged her on, far off in the Pacific "to those mosquitoey dumps that didn't even have seats on the toilets." Had she ever complained? Of course not. So why couldn't I give her the one spiritual trip she really wanted? "And besides, darling," she conned me further, "we'll be there for your birthday. The ashram is on a river. Maybe you could even fish. Please. It'll be an adventure…"

All of that.

When a friend heard we were going, he warned: "Dangerous stuff, Carney." A couple he knew had gone to "one of those places." The wife had gotten so much religion she ran off with the guru and hasn't been heard from since.

The ashram, south of Madras, India was called Shantivanam. The melody that came to mind was: "It's Only a Shanty in Old Shantytown," and I was wrong---on the optimistic side. The place looked like our tent camp on Guadalcanal that I'd tried to forget for forty years. Yes, there were palm trees here and no Jap snipers in them that I could see, but the hapless scatter of housing in the coconut grove ranged from thatch-roofed huts to abandoned surplus shacks from the British Army during the Raj time. In the miasmic heat flew or crawled every possible kind of insect, and the smell from the chow-line made me want to fast for life.

No sooner had we logged in and been assigned our penitent hutch, we were called to assembly in a tent-like torture chamber known as a yert. Rhymes with "hurt" which was the reason we'd come.

Father Bede Griffiths, the guru of the ashram, was already intoning: "The ego of western man is out of control."

Mine sure was. I felt like Alec Guinness buried alive in the tin house in <u>The Bridge on the River Kwai.</u>

"For God's sake, darling," I whispered to Teddy. "This is supposed to be my birthday, cooped up here listening to a lecture!"

"Just try it," she said savagely, "and stop talking."

Bound to silence, bound to suffer. Is heaven like this? OhmiGod!

In the yert, which was sighing in shimmering heat vapors, dozens of our fellow penitents were seated yoga style on the hard dirt floor. My bony butt groaned, and all the old horse falls that had crunched my spine began telegraphing sciatic screams down my over-length legs which weren't designed to be jacknifed into the closed position.

Teddy and I were the only American sinners who had come this far to be cleansed. We were also, I noted, the only married couple, and worse, the only Lawrence Welk generation folks, stuffed in here beside young searchers from India, England, Europe and Asia. Most of them had arrived lugging backpacks filled with worn spiritual treatises. Their bodies were so supple and suffered they could knot themselves into instant yoga positions. They thrived on moaning the chants and having sacred oils ungented on their foreheads. They had inexhaustible patience, soaking up like sponges the torturous theological tracings of Eastern religions interweaving with Christianity.

Father Bede Griffiths, whom Teddy wanted so much to hear, was clearly a brilliant and holy man. His books were internationally known. People came from far and wide for his teachings. An English Benedictine monk educated at Oxford, he'd gone to India years before because he felt that if Christianity were to survive, it would have to reconnect with the parallel roots of Eastern religions. The West should learn from them and end the dualism between body and soul that was robbing us of our wholeness.

I liked the message and believed it, if only the medium didn't have to be so gruesome. Shantivanam was no Hollywood-pretty people ashram where the guru drove a Cadillac. This was real McCoy, hardline mortification, and my flesh simply too weak for it. Probably it's the Irish in me, feeling that God intended life to be joyous, a lark, live it to its fullest. God knows, the way I live it most of the time I get suffering enough. God, I think, wants me to love myself, and for Him to take care of my flesh, not driving nails into it and hating myself for being so weak. Sure, I know I'm supposed to give Him a sacrifice in my boredom, hunger and pain. But sometimes I wonder if the world-class hurters and painers aren't on an ego trip. Look, Ma how much more miserable I can make myself than the weakling next to me. Am I doing this competition for God, or just for my pride?

In the steamy yert, I sat as if at a tennis game, wishing I were out on some sort of court I could understand. The spiritual ball would ping from white-haired Father Bede across the net to the penitents. They'd stroke it and send it back, zinging with some new ideological top spin, some detail the Upanishads had uncovered centuries before Christ. Father Bede was a helluva back court man. He returned everything. That's why it took so agonizingly LONG.

But then again, did we have anyplace to go?

I squirmed and pained and looked pleadingly at Teddy. But she had trapped me in the first row, no escape possible without clumping over the lotus folded bodies. After the first hour, she wouldn't even look at me. She was too busy writing down everything Bede said.

Along about three in the afternoon, when the temperature had cooled to 90, the endless spiritual tennis dribbled to match point. Eagerly Teddy joined the other straights and trooped off to the thatch chapel where incense burning and team chanting were already in progress.

I fled down to the riverside. It was water, all right, an expanse of trickling yellow mud about a half mile wide. Upstream, I could see whitish herds of sacred Brahman cows dumping and peeing in it. Closer, clumps of soggy Indian women were washing clothes and slapping them on hot rocks. Undoubtedly thousands of others were doing that or worse for the hundreds of miles the river flowed. Then, nearby, I spotted an Indian kid, seated in lotus position and dunking a bamboo pole.

"Fish?" I said.

"Yes," he was answering , but in the Dravidian tic of southern India was shaking his head as if he meant "no." I said, Show me some fish. A few moments later, he pulled in a minnow about three inches long. When I reached out to identify its species, he popped it into his mouth and ate it.

Scratch off blue ribbon trout stream.

By then, my thermostat was on boil. Guadalcanal was the Alps compared to this inferno. I stripped off and plunged into the kid's fishing hole. Thunk! Three inches of water for three inch fish. I felt like a mud wrestler, wallowing on TV. Swimming was impossible. All I could do was to lie on my back, cooling myself like a water buffalo, and taking pains lest a drop of the offal water from upstream touch my lips.

Scraping the mud off, I went back to our thatch barracks. It was now dusk. Some new form of chanting was going on in the candlelit chapel. To fend off the possible diaharreal effects of my swim, I rummaged out my pipe and a plastic jug of Scotch. Then, sembling I was a penitent going for meditation, I skulked back down by the riverside and began sinning again.

A sound, I whirled. An Indian nun had caught me. Sworn to silence, no words, just arching disdain in her black, bead eyes. I retreated, bowing in apology, and beat my way into a thorn thicket where I settled down to continue my secret vices. At my first sip of whiskey, beside me erupted a pair of French hippies, boy and girl, she fumbling to hike up her halter top. Possibly they were doing mutual meditation, but their glare told me that my kind of sin didn't belong in it.

I stumbled back in the darkness to the hutch bower where Teddy and I would spend my birthday night. The place reeked from the fetid toilet room that yearned for a roto-rooter to unplug its septic. No matter. I lit my pipe to kill the stink. There were not chairs, so I sat on our board bed, and the night attack began, mosquitoes humming, zapping my sweaty flesh. I was slapping, cussing the tiny window. Idiot! Close the bloody screen! What screen? Shantivanam didn't use them, as if mortification demanded getting pincushioned by insects, some as big as my thumbnail. I banged the wooden shutter closed and sulked there, gulping whiskey in the darkness, suddenly realizing I was starving. We'd had tea and scones somewhere in the uncounted hours, but where oh where was actual food?

When I groped over to the mess hall, (Teddy's correction: "a beautiful building") mess hall, lit by weak, naked bulbs, the straights were all there, operating on a schedule of events I wasn't party to. I wriggled through them and creaked down beside Teddy. We were seated on a stone floor, not a cushion in sight, legs folded under us. Father Bede was intoning Grace in several languages. Well, I thought, if silence was over, at least now we might have some sparkling dinner conversation. Then on came an ancient Victrola with a monk in some obscure language spooling out a rich doze of new theology.

Barefoot Indians and hooded nuns began passing among us carrying bowls of gruel, formed, ricey gruel that they slapped on out plates with a rusty ice cream scoop. Next came steamy bowls of brown liquid wriggling with unidentified objects resembling portions of worms. I glanced around for a knife and fork. Forget it! This was manually operated feeding, everybody bending over their tin plates and slurping the stuff into their mouths. Some were even smiling. How yummy!

I gulped. I wanted to throw up. Teddy jabbed me in the ribs. Don't be such a baby. Slowly, I put my fingers into the stool---pardon me, gruel---and my lips went on fire. Heavy duty curry, had to be to keep the concoction from rotting in the heat. Next came soggy pancake-type objects, tasting like library paste, but probably blotting up the damage done by the gorp. I was so busy eating I missed the final blessing.

Then, up again, good campers! Teddy was jabbing me. We had to help. Outside in the dark, under one tepid tap of water, we massaged our tin plates with our fingers. Saints don't need soap, but as an added sanitary fillip, we weakened enough to use greasy straw pads to hone our tinware squeaky clean. We stuck our plates in a wooden rack along with everybody else's, so you wouldn't be able to tell whose fingers you were licking for breakfast.

Teddy went off to evening vespers, which went about eleven innings and took several hours. By then, I was getting separation anxiety. I hoped she wasn't back in the toilet room again. That afternoon, just to be a devoted penitent, she'd joined some of the European hippie girls in swabbing out the latrine. They'd used straw pads which, God willing, were not the same ones we'd cleaned our plates with!

When she finally came into the darkness of our bower, I stabbed my penlight at her. She was in her nightie and smiling, as if: "Happy Birthday, darling."

Our cell was slightly bigger than, say a roomette on the Super Chief in the good old days. Our beds were two singles, two boards per, just wide enough for a very starved down martyr. And exactly far enough apart so that if I wanted to reach over and touch Teddy's weak flesh---down, boy, not here! The walls of the cell were about five feet high, and above them dark airspace up to the thatch roof. An airspace that was becoming filled with the grunts, snores, sneezes and farts of our fellow penitents, processing dinner. In their paper-thin cells, we were almost face to face, none of them being married, of course, devout women bunking with women and men with men. All but the old Lawrence Welks who should have gotten over it by now.

"For God's sake," I seethed to Teddy, crouching on hard stone beside her ear. "This is supposed to be fun? Our romantic vacation!"

"Oh, you are so spoiled, rotten spoiled!"

"Damn right I am!"

"I really want to do this, and if you can't take it, then please go someplace and leave me alone. It will be a relief not having to worry about you!"

"Don't you miss a minute of it," I said, casting myself down on my hard, lonely boards. But not for long. Bells and chanting wrenched me up at 4:30 a.m. I bailed out just in time to avoid another breakfast, by some miracle locating a car that rocketed me to a plane, and finally to a beach hotel as far away as I could get. They had window screens here, girls swimming topless in the Indian Ocean, and a big double bed that yearned for its empty half.

When it was too hot to swim, I lay under a palm tree and scrawled angry notes about the excesses of punishing religion, which I felt was keeping these Eastern and Asian peoples in bondage. I'd seen it in the Hindu temples and Muslim shrines in Singapore, where it was more important to our Malay cab driver to make his visit to Mecca than for us to make our plane. If their custom worked for them, that was their business, but to me there was a heartless futility in sacred cows being kept greasy fat while humans starved and died in the streets. Did God really want us to accept and ignore such suffering just because sects of men had invoked it in his name?

To pick up my particular Cross meant to give of my time and money, didn't it? But how? Lay my hands on the sick, as Mother

Theresa was doing? Or try to heal the brutalized, the walking wounded of our system by accepting and loving them, as they are. Or could I become an advocate to help change the system? If I had a calling, it was only to do what I believed God was telling me to do, and to be detached and not caring enough---to be stilled enough to hear.

Obviously I'd flunked the Mother Theresa part in India. I was too rotten spoiled to move the bedpans around in joy. But in groping for my own truth, perhaps my tiny voice was all I could give, and pray that God heard it, too.

With some reluctance, Teddy finally agreed to leave the saints in the ashram and come home to the sinner. As we drove away from Shantivanam, an Indian couple she'd befriended began clinging to our car. They were Biblically named Joseph and Mary. Teddy had already bought some pajamas from them for our granddaughters. But now their medical problems had become acute, Joseph trotting beside the car and imploring me with his X-rays and letters of doom from doctors. I thrust him a wad of bills. It didn't matter if he'd scammed me, I'd bought Teddy back.

I rented us the bridal suite in a small town Indian hotel, clean enough but the door handle kept coming off in my hand. We had to wait here to get out of India which you don't do readily and without pain. In the middle of the night, Teddy caught the pain. She was running a raging fever and doubled over in stomach complaints. At daybreak, I rushed her to a gloomy stone masoleum that served as the local hospital.

Because it was Sunday morning, only a small staff was on hand. The stone corridors of the hospital were filled with suffering Indian men, women and children, some appearing already dead and others going fast. Mothers were solacing wailing babies, old people were hugging each other as if there were no tomorrow. Teddy was flushed with fever, lying on a wooden bench with me stroking her head in my lap and loving her very much.

I still don't know why, but out of the mass of the afflicted, a young Indian woman doctor rescued us. She was bright and English-trained. "Oh, yes," she sighed. "The ashram at

Shantivanam. They are friends of ours, of course, and good people. But we have warned them many times: please do something about your well. It's so shallow you are drinking ground water, and God knows what that's filled with."

Whatever it was, it filled Teddy with troubles and antibiotics for weeks. But this, too, shall pass away. Going home, it began to dawn on me that perhaps I did learn something in India after all.

As we passed through the Honolulu airport, I was so starved for news from the real world, I snatched up a paper. One headline read: "Reagan Steps Up War Against Contras." So what else was new? On an adjoining page, I noted that the President was going to address the UN about the Cold War.

I scribbled off a telegram:

DEAR RONNIE AND NANCY. IN YOUR MONDAY SPEECH TO THE UN, SUGGEST YOU CONSIDER GANDHI'S CONCEPT: HATE THE SIN BUT NOT THE SINNER. DEPLORE THE EVIL OF COMMMUNISM BUT EXTEND COMPASSION TO THOSE TRAPPED WITHIN IT. NO LONGER SHOULD WE SEE THE SOVIETS AS OUR DEMON OR WE THEIRS. WE'RE ALL IN THIS TOGETHER. RECONCILIATION IS THE GENEROUS HOPEFUL VISION THAT YOU CAN COMMUNICATE AND MANKIND WILL BLESS YOU FOR. AS WE DO, IN LOVE AND PRAYERS TO YOU BOTH.

Then I bought an electric hula doll for my granddaughter and we went on home, to try again.

Ain't gonna study war no more. An old writer's prayer.

12.

You live in the context of your culture. That's not a newsflash. All of us are there. You belong to the Whole, like it of not. You can pretend that you don't care what's going on in Washington or in your neighborhood. You can try to isolate yourself from the latest bad news, whether it's a Presidential God figure being revealed as having feet of clay, or whether the anger of your society is brought home to you by a cut in pay, a rise in prices or the affront of some muted violence wreaked on you personally. You can try to bury your head in the sand. But it doesn't work.

The struggle of your spirit expresses itself through your emotions. An event "out there"---say you've lost your job or my book doesn't get published---that event is a reality. It's perfectly neutral. It is simply something that happened. But what rings a bell in your spirit is how you react to that event. What spin do your emotions put on it?

Do you allow your emotions to plunge you into the worm-eating guilt-shame-fear-anger reactions, as I did when I had my heart problem? Do you wallow in the bottom of the box and sicken yourself?

Or can you make the leap of courage into the positive energy of neutrality, willingness, acceptance and reason---and heal yourself?

Your spirit, the collective consciousness of the race, having done it all for all time, gives you an immediate yes/no answer. Something is either true or it's a lie. Your spirit *knows*, and your body acts out the knowing.

That's why you can't hide from the lies or stuff them down into yourself in denial without paying an emotional price. You have to answer the warning from your spirit by saying in effect: Yes, I've just been told a lie, but I'm not going to let my emotions whip me with this thing, flog me with anger, pride or self-hate. Stress my immune system and make me sick. Rather,

I'm going to take my power back into myself, leap to courage and spiritually rise above the neutral event out there. Make it my own, see it as part of the Whole, and motivate myself to go beyond it toward the love, joy and peace of enlightenment.

In the rising are two important steps: compassion for yourself and for the people who perpetrated the event, and gratitude for what you have---your life, NOW, in this moment, all the blessings you've been given.

But the leap to courage is a difficult one to make because our culture is constantly bombarding us with lies. Our spirit is flashing yes/no, but our emotions are muddled between the two poles. Do we believe what the powers-that-be tell us is true, or do we reject it?

World-wide experiments in kinesiology show that thoughts we hold in our minds manifest themselves in our bodies. They weaken our muscles and stress our immune systems. Negative thoughts make us sick. When our culture gives us a bombardment of negative thoughts, we don't know how to cope with them. Instead of treating some event out there as neutral, we let it "get" to us. If the world is telling us that we ought to feel guilty, bathe ourselves in shame or self-hate, we plunge down into those low emotions. If the world frightens us with violence and rumors of war, we're stuck down in fear. Or, in our powerlessness to "do" anything about it, we respond with desire---give us something better than this! Fill ourselves up with some sort of goods-gift. And when we don't get any satisfaction from it, we flame into anger, and then stiffen in pride. We deserve more than what we're getting!

Hence, the anger in the land, the war of our daily lives.

Because we've received virtually no training in the spirit, it's very difficult for us to make the leap to courage and begin our upward, positive-energy journey to the victory of surrender. It's this inability, this void of soul that leads David Hawkins, from his testing, to believe that 85% of the human race lives in the low end, death enhancing emotions.

Thus, what we'd prefer to shrug off or deny as ancient history has vital importance to us simply because of what it's done to us. It has put certain thoughts in our minds, programmed our emotions to respond to them in a negative way, while in every instant, every new event out there, our spirit is warning us: those thoughts are lies.

In my view, we're in our present emotional confusion because of three drastic changes in our personal/national identity. They have affected not only our form of government, but strike deep into our daily lives and all we hold dear.

They "get" to us in a psychic sense.

Change One: We've been raised to believe that our system of democracy/free enterprise is "of the people, for the people, and by the people." We are basically free individuals. We run our own show.

But our spirit *feels* the evidence out there and says, Not true.

What has actually happened is that our system has evolved into a new form of socialism. Instead of we common citizens owning America, the corporate state has taken it over. Corporate economic and political power has allowed the few at the top to gain unprecedented control over the many at the bottom.

Our emotional response is powerlessness, self-hate. How did we ever let this happen? And then, realizing our plight, we respond in anger. What in hell can we do about it?

Change Two: We've been raised to believe that we're ruggedly independent thinkers and have the courage of our own convictions. Nobody can sell us a bill of goods.

Lie! spirit cries!

Media-induced lust has dumbed us, the many, into passive, conformed consumers. Literally, we're goods-mouths, waiting to be fed our things.

Our emotional response is shame, guilt, anger that we've been gulled, and on the frantic heels of it, desire for more and more things in the hope that somhow they'll drown out the grieving in our souls.

Change Three: We've been raised to believe that we're a peace-loving people, having no designs on others in the world except to live and let live.

Spirit spikes it. Lie!

By creating Scapegoats, endless Enemies Out There, our government has not only terrified us and vastly profited the corporate state, but has blinded us to the deterioration of our nation and our spirits In Here.

Our emotional response is chilling fear. We are literally scared to death. Our anger bubbles over at the latest demon who did this to us. Objectify him, off him as non-human. Take him out of our way!

Pogo put his finger on it. "We have met the enemy and he is us." We're at war with ourselves about our future and our very meaning. Who are we as individuals? Which kind of America do we want? Spirit says: truth? Lie? Yes/no. Give me an answer. No wonder our emotion/bodies writhe in a torment of unknowing, stuck in the center between our negative, sickening energies and our positive healing ones.

Our emotions act out our deeply-held beliefs. Some of us are "old" Americans. We hope to go back to the country that used to be. We believe in isolation, tradition, populism. God-fearing and clinging to ethics and values that had made our nation great. "Old Americans" are usually rural, small town or blue collar workers.

Some of us, however, are "new" Americans. Just as fervently do we believe in world involvement. Our future demands that we use our power and wealth to create a single global market and community, the rising tide of which will profit us at home. "New" Americans are transnational corporations, establishment media, think tanks and most of academia.

Which side of our national psyche is right? Which will prevail? Or will the All of our spirit finally show us a way to stop separating each other into parts, and instead to join our BE and our DO into an energy-productive new whole?

Like the drunk looking for his car keys in the wrong place, we're going to have to find our own street light to see where we lost ours. Once we begin to understand what caused the darkness of the past, we may well be able to discern the shape of our future, the compassion and the healing that our spirit is trying to give us.

The changes we've lived through in the 20th century were all inter-related. The emergence of the corporate state led to the exponential growth of advertising which, when linked to the explosive power of TV created an unparalleled goods-lust. Using the same propaganda tools, it was only a short step to the creation of endless scapegoats, Enemies Out There who threatened to take away our things. From Vietnam to the womens' movement, welfare reform, civil rights, ecology, abortion, we have been polarized into a pendulum consciousness, swinging from one extreme to the other, dividing each other into Good Guy/Bad Guy scapegoats. Instead of "trampling out the vineyards where the grapes of wrath are stored," we have trampled out the middle ground where the seeds of tolerance, patience and compassion can grow.

When the stock market crashed in 1929, the ensuing Depression made us doubt the validity of our old American Dream. Free enterprise and democracy no longer seemed to be working. Because there was panic in the land and even the threat of revolution, the federal government intervened.

In his book The Critical Path, visionary Buckminister Fuller described how shortly before World War II, Franklin D. Roosevelt took steps to socialize American corporations. The publicly funded RFC gave sweetheart loans to prime defense contractors. They rarely if ever paid the money back, and furthermore balked at having to do research and development unless their expenses could be tax deductible. When FDR complied by fixing the tax code, Henry Luce of the Time empire cried foul and demanded that advertising also become a legitimate business deduction. He got his way and the war was on for the minds of America.

Under FDR and successive administrations, giant corporations were built out of massive transfers of taxpayers dollars into private hands. As Alexander Hamilton observed shortly after the Revolution, the nation had no wealth. The government must borrow its funds from the banks of rich landowners. The people were glad to pay it back in exchange for what they were getting in services. But in the Depression, when the old landowners' banking system had lost all its depositors' money, the President was voted control over the U.S. economy. U.S. citizens and their government became the last resource of wealth. For the first time in our history, the government guaranteed citizens bank accounts up to $5000. Decades later, this precedent was expanded so that taxpayers money could insure deposits in patently shaky S&L's. When oversight controls were lifted, fraudulent loans were made, uncounted billions lost, and the American people picked up the check.

According to Fuller, the Foreign Aid program was another great transfer of the peoples' wealth into a few private hands. U.S. corporations were paid by the government to produce goods for and in foreign nations. The result was 100 billion in machinery and factories that the corporations moved out of the U.S. to escape our taxation. We, the people, financed their move. We also paid 155 billion in atomic energy research that was handed over to energy companies. In the end, Fuller believed the grand total was about 6 trillion of public money transferred to 1000 U.S. corporations. Ironically, these august bodies and their lobbyists are the loudest protestors about welfare fraud, aid to unwed mothers and school lunches. Today, the amount of corporate welfare, direct subsidies to companies, reaches into the billions annually.

Our spirit spikes the lie that we as individual citizens are still masters of our own destiny. It also sees clearly that the connection between this change and the next is no accident. Now that such massive economic and political power had accreted to the corporations, it was good business for them to begin owning the windows where they could hawk their wares. This was a two-edged sword. Electronic media was more than a selling tool. It was a chokehold on politicians who needed it to sell themselves to the voters. Slowly, major corporations and news chains began engulfing and devouring most of our information sources, merging them increasingly into a single, establishment voice. When General Electric gobbled up NBC, our number one military contractor could now depict the wars that sold its products.

Advertising had been with us since colonial days when penny newspapers printed prim black notices about things we could buy. Later, the Sears Roebuck and Montgomery Ward catalogues furnished the homesteads of America. But only a short 70 years ago did radio's dramatic entertainments crash over us like a tidal wave. Almost overnight, advertising erupted into a commercial Goliath, a new god promising that we could satisfy the longings of our spirit by filling our emptiness with the purchase of things.

The goods-myth---that happiness is getting what we want---was marketed by 100 supranational corporations who buy a *hundred billion yearly of U.S. advertising.* When the shattering visual impact of TV hit the living rooms of the land, the invasion or our brains was devastating.

Electronic scientists have long known that the dancing pictures and colors of the cathode ray tube manage to shut off the left brain, which we'd formerly used to make our critical judgements. If we'd been too left brain all these years, too analytical, it was an ironic twist that TV would now catapult us to the other extreme. Joyously, we kick-started our lagging right hemisphere, the happy little kid in us who liked to have stories told to him and didn't have to bother with sequential things. In right-brain wonderland, there is no power to analyze. Without a left brain to say no, right brain became a fairy kingdom of nursery rhymes, a mindless festival that slopped finger-paints all over the real world until we couldn't see it anymore. TV gave us our escape, dangerously blurring reality into fantasy.

In the Gulf War, for example, we were confused as to which pass was in the air. Was it the pigskin in the Superbowl or one of Saddam Hussein's dreadful missiles? We were fighting (playing) both wars on the same day. Which was real, which was made up? Then came the commercials, gleaming products we had to buy if we wanted to be Somebody, a winner. The goods lust was pumped into us day and night, distracting us from distraction by distraction, morphing us into pliant consumers, getting and spending in the Global Mall.

At home, as our neighborhoods crumbled and jobs went overseas, our governors assured us not to worry. On corporate-owned TV, establishment talking heads convinced us that our problems weren't really our failed democratic myths. Instead, they were separate little fights, broken parts of our system that could be fixed. Divided and diverted, we pre-occupied ourselves with such morbid entertainments as the O.J. trial, Whitewater and the sexual follies of President Clinton. In our increasing entrainment into low end base emotions, we long for heroes, worship movie stars and the rich and the famous.

"A society in decay and denial," wrote the San Francisco Chronicle. Disconnected from our national_soul, we feel an emptiness, a sense of loss. Pressures nobody seems to understand---economic, social, spiritual---our lust for productivity becomes a race against the clock, young people particularly holding down two jobs, spending more and getting less. Life as a Master Card, grinding interest compounding. We find ourselves running faster and faster just to stay in the same place, play catch up ball so that we might *have it all.*

But things don't fill us. We barely buy them before we feel empty again, certainly only momentarily happier. It's no accident that in the Los Angeles riots, the howling mobs of the disadvantaged who smashed store fronts only took home a small amount of the stuff they'd stolen. Mostly, they hurled it out into the streets and destroyed it, as if these shiny things were the goods-dope that had hooked them. Rage at the things/fix, the god that failed.

As our confusion and powerlessness increases, we look to Washington for help. Let George do it. Get a Contract with (on?) America. But who was George anymore? Certainly not our allegedly representative government. Said John Jay, a signer of the Declaration of Independence, "The people who own the country ought to govern it." They pretty much always have in the United States, only more so now in the overwhelming new power of the corporate state.

In an age that demands a conspiracy behind every great event, the corporate state is no such thing. It's not a John Birch Society goblin of greedy CEO's meeting at the Yale Club and plotting how to take over America. Corporate executives are some of the brightest, most creative people in the nation. They're tough and smart or they wouldn't have gotten where they are. They know what they're doing and it's to serve their bottom line. That's what they were hired for. Many of them have reached far beyond their corporate realms to establish foundations and visionary programs that benefit all Americans. They love the nation that had given them so much, and they mean to give back, in gratitude.

In the composite of these executives, there is a *zeitgeist* of progress and a mind-set that is common to most of them. They've learned the hard way what works and what doesn't work. Thus, when they're confronted with some national or international problem, they often react the same way. They're not out to steal the country, only to better it. Then they go back to fighting each others' fiefdoms for market share.

They're in the political battleground to---crudely---cover their ass. That's their only conspiracy---and in the amalgam of their balance sheets, they have immense power. They don't intend to give it up.

At the 1992 GOP convention, the hotel where I stayed had rented each of its corner suites to CEO's of some of the largest corporations in America. They were in for a busy summer, for they'd next be attending the Democratic convention. It reminded me of W.C. Fields. When asked why he kept a bank account in Hitler's Germany, he replied: "Never can tell. The little sonofabitch might just win." Meanwhile, down on the convention floor, at a cost of millions drained from the party faithful, here were splendid galas, tinseled Somebodies from Hollywood, marching bands, paper hats and soused delegates tooting their horns in the balcony. They actually believed they were deciding something. When I asked a corporate power player: "Who needs these antiquated, opulent charades every 4 years---why not just scrap 'em?", he answered seriously, "No, you have to have conventions. They're like sales meetings. Pump up the salesmen, make 'em go out and sell the product. They've got to feel they're a part of it."

How does our spirit process the lie about our political parties? Weren't they established to give us a choice of evils? When Ralph Nader asked his father whether a third party wasn't a good idea, the answer was: "I'd settle for two." Now, as Nader points out and everybody knows, there's only one party, the Owners Party. It's almost as if Republicans and Democrats have been melded into Repubnocrats, a single entity, run by the money and easier to run because the power is all in one place.

How else to explain that neither party dares throw out the estimated 25,000 lobbyists scurrying around the corridors of power? Neither party dares to flush the dirty money out of elections or end the corporate welfare scams which are estimated to be costing the citizenry a staggering 456 billion a year.

The sound and fury coming out of Congress and the White House is a sophisticated game of musical chairs. Of course there are dedicated people in politics. They give up precious time with their families. They lose out on opportunities at home. They work very hard, and it's not just for the ego-stroking, the influence or power in it. These men and women honestly want to make a better country, but they're trapped in a brutal, antiquated system. Some representatives actually call their big donors "clients." Mondays and Fridays in Congress are often devoted to fund-raising for re-election. If the peoples' representatives don't go along with the owners wishes, they go home. This is how we get billions for new B2 bombers. Not only is there no enemy in sight to use them against, but the Air Force didn't even request we build them. Who did?

Again, the linkage is clear. Corporate state socialism has given us a new kind of nation. As our critical judgement is eroded, what greater myth could be conjured than the Enemy Out There, waiting to destroy us?

Another scapegoat. It's Him or Us.

There's nothing new about such deception. Shakespeare spiked the lie of it when he had Henry IV tell his son: "The best way to govern, young Harry, is to busy their giddy minds with foreign quarrels."

The scapegoat myth pushes primeaval buttons in our spirit. The great dark enemy is approaching our cave. Fight or flee! According to Rene Girard, literary analyst at Stanford, the first cultures on earth were built around human sacrifices. These rituals were essential in forming societies. They placated the gods and answered our deep longing for protection and alliance with the sacred. Human sacrifices were also a powerful bonding force. Because the sacrifice was performed by the community, the individual was absolved from guilt. The scapegoat concept became in time an ideal way out, a pressure-relief valve, a container for our personal and collective angers.

To Girard, mimetic rivalry is part of the human condition. Mimetic desire (which Madison Avenue well understands) leads to rivalry which is itself a bonding force. Our slavish conformity to the fads and fashions of modern culture spring from our basic need to imitate each other and get for ourselves what the group thinks is important.

Rivalry taken to its extreme leads to violence. When we fear there isn't enough to go around, we begin to fight for our share, and violence itself is mimetic. When we see violence, unless we have direction and use restraint, we react with violence. As proven in kinesiologic testing, when audiences see violence on TV or film, our spirit does violence to our bodies by weakening our muscles and suppressing our immune systems.

Girard suggests that when the sacrificial cult moved from the religious arena to the political, war became the ideal expressions of scapegoating.

In 1981, I caught a glimmer about how the game was being played, and I felt a fury at having swallowed it for so long. Shortly after Ronald Reagan had been elected, a prominent international financier approached me at a party. "I hear you've been an old friend of Reagan's. What kind of president do you think he'll make?"

I answered that in my experience with him, he'd always been likeable and articulate, strong in his beliefs---what you see is what you get---but whether he had the ability to run the nation and the world, I just didn't know.

The financier smiled. "Exactly what we want. A patriotic figurehead up there, wave the flag. We'll take care of the rest."

"We?" I thought.

Who was we?

Fourteen years later, in 1995, I watched a TV documentary on America's final day in Vietnam. In gripping combat footage, a U.S. helicopter lifted up from the roof of our embassy in Saigon. The Marine General who'd commanded the evacuation recalled that we'd left behind 58,000 American dead, 100,000 wounded, an estimated 4 million Vietnamese killed. The cost to us: $200 billion, in addition to our uncounted veterans still being treated for battlefield traumas or the ravages of drugs.

"All I could ask that day," the General said quietly, "and I ask it still: what had it all been for?"

Claims editor Michael Lind in <u>Harpers</u>: "It's against the rules to talk about a rapacious American oligarchy, and the suggestion that a small group of people with the most money and power just *might* be responsible to some degree for what has been happening to the country over the past 20 years."

Why the secret of the controlling elite doesn't get out, Lind claims, is that every time a politician from the left or the right proposes to "speak for the many," the nation's "better newspapers (<u>Washington Post, New York Times, Wall Street Journal</u>) react in "wrath and denial, claiming demagogy. Yes, the pundits admit, economic and social inequality have been growing in the United States with alarming results, but the ruling and possessing class cannot be blamed because, well, there is no ruling possessing class.

"The American oligarchy," he concludes, "spares no pains in promoting the belief that it does not exist, but the success of its disappearing act depends on equally strenuous efforts on the part of an American public anxious to believe in egalitarian fictions and unwilling to see what is hidden in plain sight."

As Gore Vidal put it: "Every four years, the naïve half of us who vote are encouraged to believe that if we can elect a really nice man or woman president, everything will be all right.

"But it won't be. Any individual who is able to raise 25 million to be considered presidential is not going to be much use to the people at large. He will represent oil, or aerospace, or banking or whatever monied entities are paying for him. Certainly he will never represent the people of the country and they know it."

Contract with America? "Hogwash!" says a Michigan militiaman. "We already have a contract. It's called the Constitution."

"People are afraid of the government," says an Idaho woman who refused to join a militia because she felt their views were too extreme. "McNamara comes out 30 years later and says the Vietnam war was a tragic mistake. We know the Cold War was perpetuated by the military-industrial complex. The public knows the government has lied to us."

Certainly, we ordinary citizens had little or nothing to do with the decision to invade Vietnam. So how did it happen? On an afternoon in 1963, I saw clear proof that the Washington/big business axis was setting us up for war.

The CIA, under orders from John F. Kennedy, had just destroyed the Diem government in Vietnam. Because I'd recently written an anti-communist novel, a French intelligence agent came to see me. This woman, an ex-communist, had helped author the NATO manual on psycho-political warfare. She'd also been with President Diem and Counselor Nhu the night before they were murdered, a by-product of the botched CIA coup. According to her, the U.S. had now created a vacuum of power that we could only fill by plunging American troops into a massive land war in Asia. When my friends and I heard this dire prediction, we were stunned. At that point, the U.S. had only a few thousand military observers in Vietnam, but the French agent was talking in terms of armies. Obviously, we were being duped into a war nobody wanted, and we felt strongly that the public had damn well better be warned.

The French agent spoke to a small group that I'd assembled. Some of us had Washington contacts, and Ronnie and Nancy Reagan were there too. Though Ronnie hadn't yet entered politics, he was then a TV spokesman for General Electric and had considerable visibility. We assumed that between us we could muster up press coverage on such a shocking revelation. Immediately we began calling our friends in the media. Their answer was always the same, and it stunned us.

Our story didn't jibe with Washington's story. The Administration had already launched a massive brainwash on Vietnam, and we, now, were threatening to spike the lie. The result? We couldn't get a single line in a newspaper or a sound byte even on local TV. I was so enraged that I wrote a novel dramatizing how the American people had been duped. By the time the book came out, we had thousands of troops in Vietnam, launching the major land war the French agent had predicted.

The rest is history. We plunged into an unwinnable civil war on the other side of the world because we had been propagandized to believe that the dominoes would fall and Asia would go communist.

Fall they did, the only effect being that our communist enemies became capitalists on the war riches we'd left behind, and are now hiring corporate America to build them luxury hotels and golf courses. Diplomatic recognition comes next, a booming market in which to sell our products. The U.S. lost no freedoms to evil empires. The loss was good kids who knew not why they were there, except that they'd believed our "figureheads" of the moment, "waving the flag" and "taking care of the rest," e.g. themselves.

While the Cold War was still raging, I covered a meeting of military industrial leaders in Europe. The room sparkled with generals, cabinet secretaries and CEO's of some of our largest corporations. The Pentagon had prepared a costly doomsday book showing in living color the arsenal of dreadful Soviet weaponry. Terror was being sold here. Nobody wanted to question then what has now been made patently clear. The Cold War was a fraud, the Soviet Union the ideal scapegoat for nearly 50 years. Our corporate state had manipulated him to rise and fall on cue, depending on how much our elites needed him for domestic politics---getting re-elected by being "hard on the commies," or getting re-elected by shoveling out the largesse of defense contracts into our home districts. Keep our people working, even if it was in making killing machines, and when we had a surplus, sell off what we didn't need as unfeelingly as if it were auto parts, arming our client killers all over the world.

As T.S. Eliot wrote: "Mankind cannot bear too much reality." Our spirit cannot bear it either. Since 1945, the reality of evil sold to us has been so constant and horrifying that the only way we knew to deny it was to plunge ourselves into myth. In the living color of TV, crippling our rational judgement, skillfully packaged by the masters of our media, we endured half a century of wars and rumors of wars.

The effect on our psyches was drastic. Dire news reports plunged us almost daily into the low end emotions, the bottom of the box. We lived in shame, guilt, fear, desire, anger and awful

112

pride. As for making the leap to courage---to get out of this horrible fix some way---I can only remember my own conflicted emotional responses during all those years.

I loved my country. I was a hard-line anti-communist, and I wrote my anger into books and films. During the Goldwater campaign of 1964, John Wayne asked me to write a TV special for him on the evil of the Soviet Union, and how the commies were about to take over the world. Now, I liked Wayne, "the Duke." He was out-spoken, energetic, the American symbol of patriotism. And I enjoyed him as a rough and tumble guy to work with and stay up half the night talking history and politics over more drinks than I needed. But then came the last day of filming our TV special. We'd hung a wall map over his fireplace, showing the nations the communists had taken from us colored in red. Wayne could tap them on cue and rasp out his attack on our failed foreign policy.

But in the middle of a take, I noticed that Italy and France had suddenly blossomed out just as red as their communist neighbors. "On Mr. Wayne's orders," said the art director.

"Duke," I pleaded, "you can't do that. Italy and France aren't communist."

He whirled. "Well, goddammit, "if they're not, they're gonna be any day now. Sonsofbitches, leave it colored red!"

While Duke went off to take a breather and smoke a cigar, I sneaked in the art director and had him spray paint Italy and France back to freedom's side. Duke never noticed the change.

But something was changing in me. In 1976, shortly after I'd written my American soul speech for Ronnie Reagan that he never used, I met one of "Them," a dreaded communist, face to face. He was a highly ranked Soviet who seemed as "American" as I, so skillful was he in observing our ways. He was attending a conference of East-West leaders, sponsored by David Rockefeller.

When I asked him if he thought material progress was going to bring happiness to the Russian people, his eyes caught fire and he answered, "Ah, you're talking about the spirit!"

For the next few minutes, guardedly lest his comrades catch him, he jotted down furiously with an American ball point pen the names of spiritual writers I suggested, including his countryman, Solzhenitsyn.

If he could see spirit at the soul of our wars, the missing ingredient, why couldn't we?

About that time, my sister-in-law, Marina, who's half Russian, returned to visit her family's ancestral dacha near Leningrad. Her father had been a first cousin of the Tsar. For that reason, the Soviets assigned her a dour, hardline young woman as her Intourist guide.

For days, everything was "nyet." No, Marina couldn't go back to her father's birthplace. The guide insisted that it had been burned by the Nazis during the war, even though Marina through the family grapevine knew that the estate was not only still there, but was being used as a recreation center for party big wigs.

After a frustrating trip, when it came time to leave, Marina impulsively thrust a rosary into the guide's hand. The young Russian stared at it as if it were a snake. Then, glancing around to be sure she wasn't being watched, she clutched Marina, her enemy, to her, and wept.

Godless, atheistic, materialist communists. The scapegoat we'd been sold, and had done the paying and dying for all these years.

In June, 1988, several days after returning from their epochal glasnost meeting with Gorbachev in Geneva, Ronnie and Nancy Reagan were standing with Teddy and me in the South Portico of the White House. Ronnie gripped me in his robust way. He hugged Teddy and I hugged Nancy, as if we were still kids again, roller-skating and going to dancing school in Chicago. A photographer scurried in and took our picture.

For years, by then, I'd been corresponding with Ronnie, begging him to see through the fraud of the Cold War and end it. So now that they had returned from the heart of darkness, I wondered what their reaction would be. I thanked them for their courage in making this great leap toward peace.

Ronnie smiled. "Listen, it wasn't hard to do. I've got to tell you, Otis, those Russians are wonderful people." And Nancy added, "This window of opportunity Ronnie has opened has to stay open. We've got to keep this thing going, and change the way we think about Russia."

I gasped. Was I hearing right? Russians wonderful people? What had happened to the Evil Empire? Korea, Cuban missile crisis, Berlin Airlift. Vietnam, Grenada, Nicaragua? Evil turned suddenly good? Then why all the treasure and the lives of Americans we'd flung away, defending against it? I was unmoored, even sickened.

All myth. We had died for a myth. The Russians were now, and ever had been, human beings, longing for spirit just as we.

When it was over and Teddy and I walked out on Pennsylvania Avenue, I could only whisper, "What a turnaround! Can you believe it?"

"Thank God," she said. Then even the roar of rush hour traffic seemed quieter. We sat down in an outdoor restaurant, no need for words. Just sitting still, counting our blessings.

But the war didn't end then. There was no peace dividend to give back to you and me. The war was too deep in us. We had swallowed so many lies for so long, we had hidden ourselves so deep in denial that we refused to see truth even when it struck us in the face. In the first dawn of *glasnost*, a Soviet general said wryly: "We have done you Americans a great disservice. We have taken your enemy from you. Now what are you going to do?"

The Free World was no more than a Free Market in which we could sell our goods. To make us buy into it, we needed an enemy, endless enemies, diverting us, bonding us against constant threats from Out There that would never allow us to have true peace In Here.

As historian Arnold Toynbee put it: "Military expansion is normally a result of militarism, which is itself a symptom of decline."

At the Marine Corps Air Station in Beaufort, South Carolina, the latest attack jets scream through the sky, shivering the pines and palmettos. They thunder day and night, defending us from Threat. A Defense Department sign at the air station gate reads: "The roar you hear is the sound of freedom."

We can't very well say the sound is naked aggression. In the last year, the Clinton administration has loosed those jets and many others in four undeclared, executive wars, a new record in U.S. history.

At this writing, Clinton has just launched his fifth attack, the current target a relatively new Demon Out There, the stern-jawed Yugoslavian President Slobodan Milosevic. To attack the Serbs who have been our allies in two wars---the Nazis killed a million of them---to demolition-derby a sovereign nation which poses no threat whatsoever to the security of the U.S.---what kind of plot can the Administration dream up this time?

The script is already being crafted in Washington. Adolf Hitler is now a twin. As Time magazine puts it: "Slobo is Hitler. Slobo is Saddam." The same tired fear buttons are being pushed. The U.S. has waded into the swamp of an 800 year ethnic-religious civil war, and has not the slightest idea where the exit is. For six years, the Clinton Administration has been watching Slobo rampaging through Yugoslavia, and only tut-tutting with a weak diplomatic finger. The present excuse seems to be humanitarian: to stop him from "ethnic cleansing."

Of course the brutal uprooting of innocents is heart-rending. We'd have to be callous indeed not to be moved by the human suffering in Kosovo and Bosnia before it. Who's right, who's wrong? We don't know. News film from a decade ago showed the Albanians evicting the Serb majority just as cruelly from Kosovo. Injustice answering injustice, Israeli/Arab, northern Ireland, the Congo. Religion, politics, tribal, endless ravaging over bloody ground. We yearn for both sides, all sides to begin to forgive, to live, but humanity doesn't yet seem ready for such a leap in consciousness. To watch the pitiful streams of refugees, weeping and being ripped from their land brings back terrifying memories of World War II. Every instinct in us makes us want to rush in and stop such a crime against humanity.

And yet, how do we stop it? Hasn't the same mindless violence been tearing apart many countries of the world all during our century? Did the U.S. intervene when hundreds of thousands were killed by our Indonesian ally? What about the slaughter in Tibet? Do we intervene in the presently brutal civil wars in Africa? In China, in Pakistan?

We can't be everyplace and cleanse the world. Grieve, show our compassion in aid, in humanitarian services, help raise world consciousness so that it condemns and ostracizes such butchery. Speak to forgiveness in every diplomatic effort. But to end violence by violence? When will we ever learn that it's no win? All the smart bombs in our arsenal can't blow away the hate in the human heart. We're like two adolescents in a school yard. Whether it's Slobo or Saddam, we draw a line in the dirt and dare the Demon to step over it. We tell him: "You are killing people, so now we are going to kill your people to stop you from killing people."

The day we began bombing Kosovo, President Clinton, addressing a trade union, tried to explain why we were launching still another war. "One argument he used to justify the air strikes," wrote the <u>New York Times</u>, "was that we needed a prosperous Europe that was '*a good partner with us for trading.*'"

Oops! Did he let the cat out of the bag? Trading partners are corporate business, multi-nationals, and when their bottom line is threatened, call in the troops. A day or two later, Clinton's scriptwriters deleted the embarrassing trading partner blooper and replaced it with the more marketable humanitarian theme, that we were bombing to save thousands of hapless refugees. With this or any other war, it's all marketing, selling us on the next human we have to hate.

Our high tech killing tools scream through the skies again. We're the new Roman Legions with million-dollar-a-shot missiles and F-15's. In our jet roars of freedom, do you hear one of the Pentagon briefers, one President, or one anybody ask: "How many of *them, their* boys, are we slaughtering? What are we doing it *for*?"

Isn't it to ensure that we can keep our New World Order orderly enough so that the remaining humans in it can become consumers of our goods? Once the slaughter is over, our multinational engineers will come in and profitably repair our bomb damage, as they did in Kuwait and elsewhere, and then the war weary folks can begin shopping again in our global mall. As if it all never happened and everybody's friends again. "Good partners with us for trading"---in death.

What can you and I do to spike the lie of it, and begin living the truth that our spirits cry out for? That's the real war to fight, and the choice we must make.

13.

"The 1980's were about acquiring---acquiring wealth, power, prestige. I know. I acquired more wealth and more power, more prestige than most. But you could acquire all you want and still feel empty. What power I wouldn't trade now for a little more time with my family? What price I wouldn't pay now for an evening with my friends? It took a deadly illness to put me eye to eye with the truth. But it is a truth that the country caught up in its ruthless ambition and moral decay can learn on my dying. I don't know who will lead us through the 1990's, but they must be made to speak to this spiritual vacuum at the heart of American society, this tumor of the soul."

Lee Atwater

leading Republican Party strategist during the 1980's, shortly before he died of a brain tumor.

Not long ago, an old friend visiting at the ranch in Wyoming left us his copy of the latest Sunday <u>New York Times.</u> I leafed through it idly until, in the Entertainment section, I was jolted by one headlined word: "CHOICE." To my amazement, here was a full page article on a political TV special I'd written. I'd been hired to do it by the Republican Party, the title coming to me because Barry Goldwater was their choice against Lyndon B. Johnson in the election of 1964. The theme was roughly: there are two Americas out there, LBJ's seamy and corrupt, Goldwater's clean and patriotic: choose which one you want. I'd persuaded John Wayne to do an ending for the film, and had brought in Raymond Massey as a homespun <u>Abe Lincoln in Illinois</u> narrator. He'd scrawled on my shooting script, "This is the best writing of its kind I've ever seen."

Those generous words were the high point of the whole experience which only went from bad to worse and soured me forever on the dirty pool of national politics. During the film's production, we had clandestine meetings. Memos from

Washington were slid into our pockets as if they contained secrets of the A-bomb. We didn't talk on phones because they might be bugged and our identities be revealed. Then the real bomb went off. One night, agents of the Democratic National Committee, foreshadowing Watergate, broke into our secret studio and stole one of the prints. When it reached Washington, there was a thunderclap of outrage. Herblock was doing daily lurid cartoons in the <u>Washington Post</u>, exposing the perpetrators of this vile plot. I was hiding in a foxhole in my Beverly Hills house. If my right-wing conspirator name ever surfaced, it would be curtains for whatever tenuous Hollywood career I had. Duke Wayne came down with the same dose of fear. He was on the phone, threatening me with legal action if I didn't get him off the picture. I said, "But Duke, I read you the script. You approved it." No matter. There was too much heat in the kitchen. Finally Barry Goldwater himself felt it and pulled the picture. It was never shown.

In a press conference the day after the election, reporters were given the one and only public glimpse of <u>Choice</u>. The <u>New York Herald</u> <u>Tribune</u> wrote: "This was the finest campaign material Goldwater had. It was exactly what he'd been saying throughout the campaign. It should never have been cancelled."

Now, decades later, the <u>New York Sunday Times</u> was not only running a full page of text and scenes from the film, but saying: "<u>Choice</u> changed political dialogue in America forever."

I wonder.

Yes, it was attack propaganda, but it seems now not very different from the deceptions of two administrations that had plunged us into a no-win war in Vietnam. In the film, we'd used footage of anti-war riots and black riots in the cities. This pushed a hot button, the administration furious that such protest was being revealed. To show the corruption of LBJ's cronies Bobby Baker and Billy Sol Estes, we knew that there were miles of TV news film recording their testimonies before Congress. Yet, when we'd gone to the network libraries to get clips, the administration had pulled every single foot of the film, and we were reduced to using still pictures. Moreover, ironically, the administration operatives who had broken into our studio were soon forgotten when Watergate's conspirators were revealed as being even more heinous.

Nothing has changed. Nothing is going to change when our society lives under the spell of the powerful negative energies, the attractor fields that keep us magnetized down in the darkness. Again and again, we criticize our media for affronting us with violence, kinky sex, greed and the naked power clutch of our so-called idols. But aren't we secretly them, living as we do in the low-end emotions? The media holds up a mirror to us, gives us what we want, a picture of our own face.

Any administration in Washington has immense brainwashing power. Whether it's LBJ, Ronnie Reagan or Bill Clinton, they're up there in the White House to sell the road they want us to take, and they have no shame about the means they use. PR, marketing, spin.

That's why, when the red demon scapegoat had barely collapsed, successive administrations began scanning the horizon for new Threats to divert us, and profit from. Marching in almost immediately came the Drug War, foul people Out There trying to poison our youth. Billions were stacked up in this new crusade, towering bureaucracies, all fighting for turf and lofting up new prisons across the nation in which to warehouse the superfluous victims. Next on stage was Quadhaffi, (though who remembers now why?), followed by a Cuban "beachhead" in Grenada, then Ortega's red legions in Nicaragua marching on Disneyland. Ronnie went along with the scapegoat/war system just as the others before him. Out of his deeply felt and naïve patriotism, he created the greatest debt in our history and the military juggernaut alleged to have destroyed our evil enemy.

His inheritor, George Bush I, took steps to enlist us as the policemen of the New World Order. The globe had to be sanitized, democratized, made safe, a McWorld mall in which to sell our goods. In rapid succession, we had Noriega, the ex-CIA agent transmogrified into the newest demon to hate. (He sold drugs, didn't he? Never said is the fact that the white hats we replaced him with sell even more.) And finally, another U.S. financed ogre, Saddam Hussein, "a new Hitler," rising from the desert sands. President Clinton inherited him, and like his predecessors in the White House, used the scapegoat to keep us in fear, and to wag his own dogtail with scare headlines and undeclared wars to divert us from his political troubles at home. "World Terrorism" is suddenly seeming acute. Will we be able to put a handle on it, spin it into the melding of one single demon face that can make us mad enough to fight against? Teletubbies. Be very afraid. They're Out There!

When the Saddam Hussein demon first surfaced, I attended a small meeting in a cowboy restaurant in Wyoming. One of our senators had come out to talk to us about the meaning of Saddam's sudden invasion of Kuwait. Now, this senator happens to be a friend. Our grandfathers had been coal-mining neighbors in Wyoming. The senator was at the time one of the most respected leaders in Congress, as well as being a bright, funny, dedicated American. He stood up in his honest, western way and said, "Now folks, we're not going to let Saddam get away with this. We're going to take him out in very short order. We'll absolutely flatten him in three or four days. But first I'm going to tell you what this war is about. It's not about money. It's not about oil. It's about getting rid of a new Hitler."

The woman sitting beside me sighed. She's a German, married to an American. During the war, her father and eleven of her uncles had been German generals. They were all killed. "When I was young," she whispered to me, "I was a rabid Hitler youth. We were so terribly brainwashed to die for the Fuhrer that if I'd ever caught my parents listening to British radio or the American station, I would have turned them in to the Gestapo." She clutched my arm. "But what you don't realize is how brainwashed you Americans are! That man---" she pointed at the lanky, affable senator---"is setting you up for war!"

Less than a week later, we were into Desert Storm. We tied proud yellow ribbons all over the nation. We incinerated Iraqi objects in vague numbers, perhaps a hundred thousand, two hundred thousand, who knew or cared? It was our oil, and our money. Would we have slaughtered a demon nation the size of Kentucky if its only products had been, say, ham or racehorses? But no, this was Hitler! What a button to push! We carried out our attack because the fear myth of the scapegoat had again been sold to us. Throw in chemical weapons, nuclear weapons, and the cherry on top, another madman---all the fear-myth ingredients were pumped into our minds---and we were cringing in such terror that we never even questioned them.

The Saddam scapegoat is important because like the movie line, "Fletch lives," Saddam has been made to live in our psyches from 1991 to the present, and probably will keep being pulled out of the goblin closet well into the foreseeable future. He is terror-on-demand whenever he serves the purpose of our managers. On New Year's Day,`1999, when President Clinton was recreating at a seminar in South Carolina, a frightened woman told the local newspaper: "We can protect the President while he's at our Marine Corps Air Station, but once he's so exposed out on Hilton Head island, one of Saddam's missiles could kill him."

How was that again? Tiny, landlocked Iraq is firing a missile a third of the way around the world to take out our President? Shades of Danny Ortega marching on Disneyland. Play it again, Sam. Saddam is the state of the art scapegoat. Lest we forget, we had shoveled weapons to Saddam for years. He was our ally. Only a few months before Desert Storm, U.S. News and World Report ran a photo of George Bush praising Saddam's Iraq on its "democratic progress."

What about Saddam "gassing his own people?" His dreaded germ warfare? According to a congressional intelligence committee, the U.S. had decided to arm the luckless, landless Kurdish tribesmen so that they could "sap the resources of Iraq," and we could please our then-friend, Iran.

"This policy," writes Harpers, "was not imparted to our clients, the Kurds, whom we encouraged to continue fighting. It was not imparted either to the American public and the Congress. We'd armed the Kurds, let them fight for us, and after they'd served our realpolitk purpose, we dumped them."

Saddam got the signal. On the next day he moved in and according to the Bush administration "began gassing the Kurds." But did he? An Army War College report shows that only Iran, not Iraq, had cyanide gas, of which the Kurds died, because the casualties lips were blue, a symptom of it. On another instance of

Saddam's supposed gassing, the Army report concludes: 'We find it impossible to confirm that gas was used."

And yet, writes Harpers, "the CIA director at the time happens to be the same man who now wants you to believe Saddam is suddenly 'worse than Hitler.'"

Foreign policy scholar Seymour Melman, professor emeritus at Columbia University and Chairman, National Commission for Economic Conversion, asked at the time: "Why is Bush rushing down the path to another wasteful, destructive war? Oil supply is no issue. The Administration is crying wolf about oil. The real objective in the Persian Gulf is to achieve a permanent military presence to dominate the area. This would justify a continuation of enormous military budgets that ensure the prosperity of military industry, as well as the power of Bush, now the CEO of the military-industrial complex. Such policies have gutted the U.S. economy. The war economy from 1949-1989 used up $8.2 trillion of resources of every kind---this exceeded the value of all U.S. industry and infrastructure which was $7.3 trillion."

Our war against Iraq demonstrates the objectifying of enemies that we've practiced since World War II. Wrote the Washington Post, "When General Powell says that he will 'kill it,' he doesn't really mean the slaughter of Iraqi human beings, only the Iraqi 'army.' He's killing an 'it.' Not a 'them.' And 'it' doesn't bleed or moan when bombed by U.S. pilots. No loved ones to grieve at home. The first casualty reports suggest thousands of Iraqi 'its' have gone down."

Our spirit winces. War has been an integral part of human history. We've always fought each other. Yet now, in the world-wide emergence of a higher consciousness, we're slowly beginning to realize our interconnectedness with all life. Our spirit knows that those slain "its" are us. Why are we destroying a part of ourselves? Aren't we being made to live a lie against human nature? This is a new awakening, "just" war and murder now bleeding into each other when we wipe out civilian populations.

If respected generals are free to kill an 'it,'---this is their job and they do it well---where is the separation between war and peace? Beside Powell's front page statement was the story of a

14 year old boy who had just shot and killed a 15 year old---over a girlfriend.

Said Thich Nhat Hanh, the Vietnamese Buddhist monk nominated for the Nobel Prize, "The roots of war are in the way we live our daily lives. The way we develop our industries, build our society, consume goods. We cannot just blame one side or the other. We need the vision of inter-being---we belong to each other. Every side is 'our side'---there is no evil side."

Why can't we see the truth? Because, simply, we buy into the age-old brainwash. We bond together against the Enemy Out There. Just as in the Vietnam tragedy, when I'd tried to expose the deception being foisted on us, in the Gulf War I wrote newspaper articles questioning U.S. motives. Earlier, I'd done some writing for the <u>Los Angeles Times</u> syndicate. In a short op-ed piece, I presented some of the facts that had been buried in our rush to war. A day or two later, an apologetic editor called me. "I loved what you wrote," he said. "I agree with it, but unfortunately we can't run it."

"Oh? How come?"

"We've had orders from up top: we can't print anything about the Gulf War unless the spokesman is a senior government or military official, which you are not."

Shortly thereafter, I talked to a former Time editor-in-chief. I congratulated him that the magazine had the guts to print an anti-war editorial by a woman writer who's a respected radical. He sniffed: "If I were still running the magazine, she wouldn't have been in there."

During the last hours of the Gulf War, the Rotary Club in a small California town asked me to address them and give them "the other side." When I walked into the room, I knew the game was over. Many of the Rotarians were friends of mine, fellow cattle ranchers or men I'd hunted quail with. One of them came up to me and proudly displayed the new jacket his wife had made for him. It was a silken rendition of Old Glory. He glistened with stars and stripes. Yellow ribbons were on the tables. I'd been scheduled to talk for a half hour on the brainwash America was getting, but just before I took the dais, there was an apologetic interruption. A senior girl from the high school had been invited in to recount the progress of the youth program they'd been working on. Poor little thing was shy, fumbling out a bunch of numbers. When she finished, I had five minutes left to show why we were burying our heads in the desert sand.

Those were all good, patriotic folks, but they just didn't want to hear. Justice, reason and truth are the first casualties of war. Because of the drenching Washington gives us, we all become guilty bystanders to crimes against humanity. Seduced by our way of life, mythed by our media, blinded to human compassion by our preoccupation with our own little agendas, we rushed on to live the lie of the scapegoat one more time, and count on it--- we're not done yet with Saddam, Slobo or the next demon.

So now at home, we wonder why our preachers, politicians and pundits mourn the loss of our family values and the violence riddling our neighborhoods. We're good and peaceful people. How come this? But deep down in us, our spirit knows the truth. We ARE violence.

This is our war in ourselves that we refuse to give up. As taxpaying citizens, our dollars have trained the death squads in Latin America, Africa and the Orient. With the exception of a few nuns and priests testifying before Congress, we've mostly turned a blind eye to the slaughter of innocents. It's no accident that we always support the elites in the third world nations. All the power is in one strongman or just a few---centralized, easier to deal with in a business sense. The elites maintain order and the status quo. They protect our interests against the specter of a disorganized populace seizing control of their nation and lopping off a tentacle or two of our investments. Populist pressure cries out to nationalize, as if it's "their " bananas now, or "their" oil. Didn't we say exactly that to Saddam Hussein. The riches under his sand were not his at all. It was "our" oil. Our corporations had put money into it.

General Smedley D. Butler, with two Congressional Medals of Honor, was the most decorated Marine in our history. He'd fought from the Boxer Rebellion in China down through all the Banana Wars in Haiti and Central America. Testifying before Congress in 1931, he said that he'd helped save Standard Oil in

China, and Brown Brothers Harriman in Central America. "I've spent 33 years in active service," he concluded, "most of my time being a high-class muscleman for Wall Street and the bankers. I was a racketeer for capitalism."

Butler had blown the whistle, questioned the holy writ of capitalism. The system court-martialed him and kicked him out. "To have worked for 33 years," he wrote, "with a spotless record, to have been awarded two medals of honor and sixteen other decorations for service to my country---and then to wind up my career in the Marine Corps by seeing my flag hauled down and being placed under close arrest like a criminal---well, it was a pretty savage blow. But we live on momentum. If you stop going, you are finished. My momentum and enthusiasm will still carry me forward. There's plenty of fight in me yet."

Where are the Butlers and Gandhi's of our time?

They're not many of them around to protest the injustice and loss of our freedom in the Drug War. The so-called War on Some Drugs is simply another lie playing on our irrational fears. Of course drugs are bad, but what about tobacco and particularly alcohol which wreaks ten times as much havoc as drugs in our society? Why are some mind-altering substances legal and some not? Valium and Prozac have far more adherents than cocaine, and the fountain of youth of Viagra seems sure to catch up. But with despised "hard drugs," our frenzy to defeat another Enemy Out There has led us to take a medical/spiritual problem and militarize it. Turn a victimless crime into a war, with multi-billion dollar "drug defense" budgets creating an ever-mushrooming bureaucracy which has not won the war yet, if indeed it was ever intended to. Human nature being what it is, mankind has always sought transcendence to altered states. When there is no escape to the spirit, and no future in ravaged lives, drugs seem like the only way out.

The single major victory of the Drug War is the number of prisoners it has taken. It has gotten pathetic escapers, derelict, crime-ridden misfits out of our way temporarily. We have warehoused more black and brown people in our prisons than any country in the world. The so-called "police states" of Russia and China don't even come close.

The Drug War fails and will continue to fail, just as Prohibition did, because our policy is based in the death-enhancing energies of fear, anger and pride. To succeed in healing, it would have to rise into acceptance, reason and compassion. As the American Medical Association said, "It's a problem for the physician, not the policeman."

Our orgy of violence has shattered family values and cultures not only at home but all over the world. Our kids see what we're doing. They cheer and envy our smart bombs. Their fingers skitter over the kill-kill-kill buttons on their video games. They flock to the next film that is bloodier than the last. They're so deadened to gore that they demand having it ratcheted up ever more obscenely to get any thrill at all.

How do we end this cycle of man's inhumanity to man, and mostly, to end the psychic war that's tearing apart our souls?

There is truly only one way.

One by one, in lifting ourselves to a higher level of consciousness, we end our war by re-conceptualizing the whole of us, the interconnected All of our meaning on earth. We heal our national soul.

We'll never do it by the parts-thinking of Newton and Bacon. Like the old song, "You push the first valve down, the music goes round and round, oh-oh, oh-oh and it comes out here." There are too many parts. Try to fix one and the music comes out somewhere else. We slap an embargo on foul old Castro and bankrupt the wheat crop of Canada, our largest trading partner. The Department of Agriculture tries a new pesticide on cotton and wipes out the black-footed ferrets, an endangered species. Yearly, dozens of respected scholars write articles or books describing the repairs our system needs. The points are usually valid: we restructure the tax code or the way we elect our leaders. We re-make Social Security or Health Care. We argue and divide and fight over methods. Nothing changes. So how then do we cope with our structural decay?

We stop treating the symptoms, and instead focus on the core disease. The cancer of our soul.

All the remedies in the world for putting Humpty Dumpty back together again haven't worked in the past and won't work now.

Only in our spirit, the soul of us, lies the holistic answer.

Where is it telling us to go? Can we listen to that? Can we hear, and begin to act on the change in ourselves that our spirit demands?

Wise men, living on the spirit level, have already shown us the way. "The wars, cataclysms and plagues that convulse human society," wrote Thomas Merton, "are in reality the outward expression of a hidden spiritual battle. To be consciously and spiritually committed to the worldly power struggle in business, politics and war is to founder in darkness, confusion and sin."

Doesn't the shoe fit us? Isn't that where we live? Isn't the war of our lives our worldly power struggle in our business, our politics and our actual killing wars?

But spirit sees another side of the coin. The hope that as more and more of us rise toward enlightenment, we *are* changing ourselves in ways we never dreamed of before.

"The turn toward inward development," wrote novelist Alexander Solzhenitsyn, "the triumph of inwardness (being), over outwardness (doing), will be a great turning point in the history of mankind, comparable to the transition from the Middle Ages to the Renaissance. There will be a complete change, not only in the direction of our interests and activities, but in the very nature of human beings, a change from spiritual dispersion to spiritual concentration. This ascension will be similar to climbing onto the next anthropological stage. No one on earth has any way left but upward."

Upward is where our spirit lives. It is there that we must go, and indeed we are headed exactly there at this very moment.

The mystic, Ingo Swann, who predicted the end of the Berlin Wall 18 months before it happened, is world-renowned for his ability to tap into consciousness. He writes: "1998 will be the year in which the future becomes irrevocably detached from the past. The completeness of the failure of most 20th century systems, mindsets and affiliated institutions will be clearly visible by then. Twentieth century system failures will result in a great sense of betrayal and great, unifying anger. It is out of this great anger that the centralizing, re-empowering highest values of the third millenium will arise. These values will not remotely resemble those of the 20th century."

Will it happen here? Can we make ourselves into new people, leaping to the courage of our spirit, so that we may face, cope and handle the challenge of our future?

We did it before, and we can do it again. In 1776, what people called America was a captive nation, enslaved by Great Britain in a system of economic and military domination. But despite how unjust and brutal the system was, the vast majority of Americans were afraid to give it up. It was the devil they knew. But then, like now, change was in the air. Only eleven percent of the colonists were open to these winds of change, yet the rising spirit of that eleven percent made the American Revolution happen.

In kinesiologic testing, The Declaration of Independence measures at 700, a document exploding with enlightenment. The words of Lincoln's Gettysburg Address had exactly the same liberating effect on our psyches. We were indeed at that time "the last best hope on earth."

What about today, now? What we haven't yet processed is the startling fact that despite our national malaise, recent polls show that an estimated one-quarter of us have already risen high enough into spirit, into the healing emotions, that these people are seeking a society of spiritual enlightenment and a total break with the old mindsets and systems. Such men and women are already beginning to live their search for truth in myriad ways. They're going into their souls so that they can let go and let God, whether it's in addicts anonymous groups in every town in the land, or in thinking locally in community betterment, or thinking globally in protecting the environment that belongs to us all.

They're just saying no to the bondage of the past, and the atrocities of violence, the induced fears and wantingness that are eating away their souls.

The ancient enslavements of mankind---divine right of kings, degredation of women, slavery and imperialism---were all ended when a small percentage of humans rose high enough into enlightenment that they threw out the failed systems of the past.

"Salvation lies in the effort," said Gandhi, "not the attainment. Full effort is full victory."

Out of that thinking, he ended the British Empire's enslavement of India.

He won his victory by surrender.

So shall we, when enough of us, one by one, learn the ways of letting go, and letting the God of our spirit show us where we have to be.

14.

Think of your spirit as the flame of a candle. Better still, think of your body as the candle itself. It's a fairly mundane container, encircling a wick that runs down it like a spinal cord. The more the flame of your candle burns, the more your physical body melts away. Eventually, you come to realize that the spirit flame of the candle is the only worthwhile part of the apparatus. Your candle body is perishable, but your spirit flame continues to give you warmth and light as long as you can keep it burning.

Wise men and women throughout the ages have seen a meditation in the flame. You can stare at it and hypnotize yourself with your connection to the eternal. As long as you can keep that flame burning, you have the warmth and light to keep you alive. Moreover, the stronger you can keep your flame burning, the more warmth and light you'll bring to all humanity. "Better to light one candle," someone said, "than to curse the darkness."

But it's bigger than that. The flame of your spirit is connected to the flame of every living thing. The unfolding of all life needs you. Your spirit flame is your meaning. You want to offer up the full brightness of it every day to the power that is greater than you because it gave you life and gave all life.

That's what your surrender is. Lift above the mundane candle that will melt away. Forget the smoke and the wax dribbling from the lowly thing. See only the flame, and offer up the best of it, the brightest you can keep it, to the sacred life force, in which you are a tiny irreplaceable light.

You dare not let your spirit-flame flicker and die.

I'm no monk. I'm far from being an intellectual. I'm not even devout. I'd rather fish or ride a horse than pray. And I squirm my way through most of the churching I've ever had. So perhaps, like you, I'm just an ordinary civilian who has lost his way in the soul-shredder of now.

The storms from without, and mostly from within me, keep

flickering my flame. Damn you, I say, God give me the courage to step out of the way. Use my ego to get me out of bed in the morning, but restrain it so that it doesn't totally possess me. Let me just stare at my flame and breathe it strong and bright and glorious enough so that it will be the one thing of beauty that I can offer up, and surrender away. Letting go and letting the God of my spirit be free to guide me.

Wherever we together shall go.

That's the only victory I know.

So how, you say, as I say to myself a hundred times a day, do you train yourself to win the battle of your soul?

If you haven't learned it in church or family or school, what are the rules for making it happen? (Not making, that's Do. Letting, that's Be.) Letting the you that is you and I show us the how and the why of getting ourselves out of our unplayable lie.

I've learned some ways, the hard way.

I dare not impose them on you.

In sum, they come down to one thing.

You have to surrender your ego.

You have to cut loose from your agenda. Give up the big image and the power and the glory and the Do of it.

Just for this precious moment in your spirit---just let go and Be.

Try it, you'll like it.

Go back to the flame. You want to offer up the brightest flame you can give to humanity and the life force. So what is this now? What is flickering it? What ill wind is ripping at it, making it splutter and even go dark?

Chances are, it's the storm in your head. You're meditating on the wonder of the flame, you think, but hell no. Wild thoughts have swept into your consciousness, beginning to sting it like hailstones. From those thoughts rattling in your head, those negative loops moaning in your echo chamber like a tape deck gone mad, your emotions are already sending signals to your body candle. Soft it goes, like your muscles. Weak it goes, like your immune system.

You're sickening yourself with the ideas you're holding in your mind. You didn't ask for those ideas, but damn if you can shut 'em off, either. The old black magic has got you, the old black habits in the bottom of your box.

You're supposed to be sitting or kneeling, staring at your incredible flame, but now you're starting to weaken it, snuff it, literally drowning it out by sucking yourself back down into the low-low emotions, the Do world you've lived in all your life.

Do? Do what? Well, pluck down one of those hailstones rattling in your brain. What do we have here? Shame/thought, isn't it? The argument you had with your wife this morning. Guilt, too, you're a bummer, all she's given you. Hate that worthless sonofabitch that's you.

But no way. Pick up the next hailstone that's rattled in. It has Pride written all over it. Goddammit, you've busted your ass all these years to rise up to the top, a fine job, provided the best of the best for your wife and kids. And besides, what was the rumor going around the office yesterday? Big directors meeting this noon. The word is, they're going to bump you up to v.p. and director, too. Your salary goes up 20 percent and you get a bundle more stock options. Paradise now! Take that brochure out of your desk. Vacation in Tahiti. By three o'clock this afternoon, the boss will be walking in and you'll have islands and palm trees and slinky Polynesian girls in your hip pocket.

Suppose he doesn't, though? In that sealed-up boardroom, somebody who envies you or hates you cuts your throat. The raise goes to another guy over in Sales. The boss never opens your door and slaps you on the back. So now a new blast of hailstones. All FEAR! Why are you lying to yourself? You know the company is downsizing. Your job could be moved to Taiwan. The boss says, Sorry, pal, but we wouldn't ask you to travel--- your kids in school here, your wife located two blocks away from her parents. Anyway, we need Chinese executives out there. Best brains you could buy, for a third of what we pay you. We have to compete in the world marketplace---

Amen amen I say to you. Get lost.

Look at your spirit flame. Fear has shriveled it into a tiny flicker and a wisp of smoke.

Anger now! Blow it the hell out! This spirit crap doesn't work, never did. Remember when you were a Marine what your old gunny sergeant used to say: "Fuck 'em all and save six for pallbearers!"

Stare at the flame with tears in your eyes. It's not there anymore. Gone dead. You're an olding, self-hating sonofabitch, weeping in the darkness.

Buddy, can you spare a match?

That's courage talking. Give you a light. In the light, you'll see that none of it matters a damn, does it? Just get up off the floor and start trying again. We're all out there, rooting for you. We need you, keeping the juice on, win or lose.

But why is it so hard to make that leap to courage? To keep our spirit flame alive?

Doesn't it come down to our lack of training in the spirit, and our surfeit of entrainment into the powerful negative electricities of old bad mental habits? Stinkin' thinkin'. We allow our thoughts, our perpetual loops of doing running in our heads, to do us in.

Thomas Merton said: "When I chop wood, I chop wood." In other words, he had trained himself to focus totally on the task at hand. He was living in the exact NOW of it. In this precious present, he was living in havingness. He had everything he needed. Everything is perfect just as it is in this moment.

Live there where he did in the exact now, and you have taken your power back into yourself. Every past guilt you allow to cross your mind reduces the power of your spirit flame. Every fear of the future you allow to cross your mind flickers it still further.

Analyze your thoughts in your meditative moment. Isn't every one of them connected to your ego in some way? What you failed to do in the past is all ego. You're telling yourself you should have been perfect. What you want to get for yourself in the future is all ego. Pride! You deserve the promotion! You're a winner! You've got to be a winner. You are forcing your way to what you think is victory, putting yourself in the hands of other people or other events that will give you what you want.

Your low-end emotions are trapping you in the darkness of wantingness. In trying to force your victory, you have given your power away---and mostly you have tortured yourself with fantasies. You have cut yourself off from the only peace any human can ever know. You have deprived yourself of the happiness of the exact now where you have not one fear in this instant, not one memory. You have it all in this moment, and all is perfect just in who you are and where you are. You have life. You have meaning.

This is the power of surrendering your ego. Be who you are NOW. Let all the rest go. Let it happen. Just be.

I think T.S. Eliot said it best. "Teach us to care, and not to care." The care is Merton chopping wood. He is going to put the power of his full spirit flame into that pile of logs. He is going to chop like hell, give it his all, feel the joy of his body at work, smell the pungent wood and freshness of the air. He has everything just now. That's his care.

And his not care? Nobody's going to pay him for the cord he's chopped. Nobody is even going to pat him on the back. He has cut himself off from any worldly reward. He has already had it, just in the joy of being in the peace of the now, and the knowing that his caring very much has combined his being and his doing into a job well done.

He has literally recreated himself in the moment of his work, and become whole. The power of his yin and yang, fused in eternal harmony, is the surrender he offers to the sacred of all humanity.

Sometimes I long in my dreams for a technology that would help us live in the now, that would kill off every negative thought that crosses our minds, and would properly insulate us from our driving, doing ego. Frankly, I think of the gimmick as a "thought-zapper." Say it's a pair of clear eye-glasses that has a little chip built into the nose piece. That chip is a wondrous thing that can read the electricity of our consciousness. The chip also has a mild electrical charge in it that zaps our nose whenever we drift away from the now.

Every time a past or future thought, worry, fear drifts in, the zapper reads it and zings us on the nose, as if saying: That's ego! Spike it, let it go! The zapper can't be fooled. Every time we allow a negative thought of guilt, shame, apathy, fear, desire, anget or pride to sneak into our consciousness, the shock stings us back to the reality of the now---that we have everything we need in this precious moment---don't screw it up, dare not weaken your spirit flame.

Then the zapper goes a step further. Like a dog with a shock collar on, when the dog gets too close to the electric fence, or rushes wildly too far afield, the shock reminds him of his boundaries. With a yelp of pain, he realizes he has to come back to who he is, where he is. And then, if he makes the leap to courage, that he can face, cope and handle the realities of his boundary, the shock suddenly stops. He's a happy little pup now, and minds the wishes of his master.

Our imaginary thought-zapper could reward us by a similar clarity of vision. Should we make the leap to courage, and then up through detachment,, willingness, acceptance and reason, the world of our present moment of havingness suddenly becomes brighter and clearer. We see, feel and smell the beauty of this moment of life. We're in a state of grace in our knowing that we're invaluable in our treasure-world of havingness. Nothing can touch us here. The place is benign. The God of life is in his heaven and everything is coming up roses. So our next step upward to full enlightenment is not a step at all. Everything is a seamless whole. We simply arrive into the love, joy and peace of the moment and try to live there as best we can, letting those high emotions heal us.

Of course there isn't a thought-zapper and never will be. Yet, maybe it's not even necessary. Once you learn the technique of rising as much as possible into the healing emotions, your thinking pattern more or less goes on automatic pilot. Your consciousness becomes increasingly alert to any threats that are trying to sicken it and weaken the precious flame that you've been born to give to humanity.

What are those threats?

In my own case at least, the capstone of the pyramid of ego doom is money. Pull out the capstone and the whole rotten structure falls in a heap. Then you can pick your way through the spiritual rubble and find out who you really are.

It's no secret to you, I'm sure, that we're money sick in America, and I suspect you're just as sick of it as I am.

Money-think is about to destroy our country. The only way you can stop that destruction is to stop it in you.

It's not an easy challenge. Neither you nor I created the money-climate. We didn't intend to have money crammed down our throats, to be forced to live money until we become money. If you have money, you're Somebody, worth something. You can buy stuff at the mall. If you don't have it, you're Nobody. Occupant. No value as a human being. No thing.

Small wonder that we worship it so. It's the only god we have left.

But what counts more, our money or our lives? When you rise to the higher, healing emotions, you realize that money is irrelevant. It's not at all why we've been put here. It's not truth. It's only a concept, an old shell game that has provided a millennia of convenience but has also been a tool used against free men and women by others who want to control them.

The economists will tell you that you have to have money because it's the only organizing principle for any society. But that's not true. Money is a dividing principle because it creates winners and losers. We haven't always had money. Primitive societies got along very nicely without it. If they needed things, they bartered. They traded goods but mostly animals, wealth you could eat. When they took their trade to the sea, it became too complicated to lug animals around in the holds of ships, so the primitives began using markers to represent the animals. Coin of the realm, and later gold. But these societies didn't turn money into their god like we have. Survival of the community was what mattered. Then, about 1500 B.C., someone figured out that if I could call this mine and you could call that yours, and mine was worth more than yours, then I could get you to work for me so that you could get some of mine. Getting, that's what money is about. I could enslave you for the value of a bull's head on a tin coin.

So the money myth grew. Without the inducement of it, we were told, without some personal gain in it for you, you and everybody else aren't going to want to work. Human nature has to have some kind of motivation.

The best motivation for work is love. You loving your work,

and me, mine. It's your expression of your uniqueness. It's your prayer, your meaning. What do we spend our lives pursuing and never getting enough of? It's not money, never has been. It's love. What's a paycheck but someone stroking you, giving you love?

Our spirit knows that love is coded into us in our longing for joy and peace. It's no accident that in thousands of accounts of near-death experiences, all the experiencers were overwhelmed by the purity of love showered upon them by the brilliant light on the edge of the beyond. A majority of them reported an instantaneous life review in which they were shown all the actions and thoughts of their lives in a stunning block of knowledge. It happened because the great data base of our consciousness had stored those moments in the overlapping hologram of time past. There was no judgement day here. No greater power castigated them for the way they had lived. All they felt was a tremendous sorrow that during their time on earth, they had not loved enough.

Compare that incredible knowing to the dead paper of money--- one has eternal meaning, the other, ephemeral, dead leaves blowing away in the fall.

Yet if money is the main threat to your spirit flame, how do you turn your back to it, shield your candle from its ill wind?

"God," observed Will Rogers, "must have had a low opinion of money. Look at the people he gave it to." But again, it's not God's fault, or the peoples' either. Money has been something *done* to us. In the historic cycles of our growth, money has pervaded us until the echo chamber of the media has magnified it into the most important thing in the world I saw the change overtake my own father, Roy. His immigrant father, Will, having come from nothing, regarded money as a blessing he'd never expected. He built jobs and careers with it, and he gave it away unfeelingly to his family and charities. In his humble simplicity, he was an easy going, genial man. But when the Depression struck and Will's health failed, Roy had to take over the role of the hard guy and go through the anguish of dismantling Will's empire. During this time, I think, the money clutch hit him. At all cost, we had to hold onto what we had. Roy was a good man;

he was a fighter. Whenever he saw injustice, he had the courage to speak up and act against it. During the Depression, the Sinclair Oil company engaged in a stock swap that would have fleeced its investors, including Roy. So, on behalf of himself and other shareholders, he took the giant to court, fought it in a nasty trial for three years, and finally won. Even as a kid, I worried about the strain on him. The effects of the money war never left him.

Years later, when I introduced him to a friend who'd been in the Peace Corps, Roy frowned, trying to process it. Finally he said in amazement, "Peace Corps? Why, there's no money in that, is there?"

As a boy, I pretty much grew up with horses, raising colts, breaking them. I loved them, particularly the sleek graceful thoroughbreds who could make it to the racetrack. Much to Roy's dismay, I'd sneak off to nearby Arlington Park and bet my two bucks on some dreamboat who just had to win. Will's sister, my great aunt Nora who lived with us was always up for a gamble, so she'd slip me a fiver to put on something of my choice. But even then, Roy's anger at my antics puzzled me. He despised the racetrack and any form of gambling, yet he was known as a shrewd investor. When the stock market began to recover from the Depression, he'd say, "Buy the good companies, and when they go down, buy more of them." So, like most of his peers, the ups and downs of the market became his coin of the realm. Many of his friends and golf partners were stock brokers, affable guys who were always watching the ticker and who had irrepressable optimism: every day it goes down is just one day closer to when it goes up.

As a kid, I couldn't figure it out. If stock brokers were considered upstanding citizens and racetrack gamblers were louts, weren't they both doing the same thing? What made paper ponies any more respectable than beautiful live ones, running for the roses with the look of eagles in their eyes?

I never got an answer until I was leaving home to make a new life in the West. One of my friends was a stockbroker. I put my arm around him and told him I was going to miss him. He looked at me with ice in his blue eyes. "You will like hell. All the years you've lived here, you've never given me a cent worth of business."

Not long thereafter when I was writing and producing for Jack Webb of <u>Dragnet</u> fame, we had two shows on NBC. At a friend's house one night, I happened to be playing bumper pool with the president of the network. In a moment when we were racking up the balls, I felt emboldened enough to say to him, in effect: Look, TV is so powerful, it can accomplish so many great things, wouldn't you want to be known as the president of the network that takes the lead in doing programming of lasting or educational value, rather than this diet of adult comic strips and laughtracks of dreck?

He was chalking his cue. His head snapped up. "I want to be known," he said, "as the president of the network that makes the most money."

One more blow against the spirit flame of your candle.

A friend will be staying with me out in the sagebrush of our ranch in Wyoming. Suddenly he'll start looking bereft. Don't I have a <u>Wall Street Journal</u>? Nope. Horror! No <u>Journal</u>? How can I exist without it? Sorry about that, I say. It's my loss, I'm sure. The <u>Journal</u> is an outstanding paper . I'd had respected friends on the staff, one of whom ran a story of mine from Mexico and got it into the Congressional Record. Still, out in my remote land where men and women occupy themselves mostly by jogging along on horses behind the tails of cows, the <u>Journal</u> is hardly a must-read. So how come, I thought, it now seems to have risen to the level of scripture?

When I was working on a daily paper right after World War II, if there was a WSJ around, none of us in the newsroom were aware of it. A few obscure financial sheets were being published someplace, but we wouldn't dream of looking to them for news. The top Guild salary for a reporter then was $450 a month which after the house and car payments were cut out left only pennies for frivolous stock playing. Then almost overnight, as the corporate state exploded, the money god roared and created unto himself his Bible. The gospel according to Dow Jones. Unless you got your nose inside the money tent, sniff out what the big boys were doing, you'd miss your chance to go for the jugular of life. Naturally, the gray pages of stock listings expanded and began to meld into politics, foreign affairs and the effect on the market of the latest Enemy Out There. Stock pickers and corporate carnivores became the idols of the day.

One of them I happen to know and love as a human being. When young people particularly hear that we're friends, their eyes widen in awe. No, they're not trying to get me to filch stock tips from him. They don't even beg for his financial advice. All they want is to adore him from afar because he is seated on one of the thrones of the money god. He knows how to make the stuff work. They want to rub the belly of the Buddha, even if they have to do it through a mere commoner like me.

Would that our currency be printed with a tobacco-like warning: "This substance is hazardous to your emotional health."

Because it is, unless you have the detachment of a saint and or know the spiritual techniques of not letting it get to you. Money plunges you into the bottom of the box. It flickers your spirit flame like nothing else in the world. It's even more powerful than sex. If you don't get money, you're into shame and guilt. If you can't get money you're into fear, and if you do get some you're now into worse fear that you might lose it. If you dream about getting it and all the neat things you can buy with it, you're gulping like a greedy greyhound at desire. And if you do finally get it, you puff up like a peacock in the splendor of pride. Look, Ma, no hands. See the me that beat all the rest and did this. Trophy time. Build the second or third vacation mansion, get the Ferrari, the yacht, the jet, how about a new trophy wife? Lives of the rich and famous, whiling your days away trying to figure out where in the world you can go next to play, soaring off into wantingness, havingness gone, no here and now, only trying desperately to figure out how to stop boring yourself to death.

They used to warn us in catechism to avoid the near occasion of sin. I thought it meant girls. It usually did, back then. But today's sexpot wears a see-through green dress that will do you in every time. Is there any antidote? Of course. Rising into your positive emotion of neutrality, detach from money's sticky fingers. Rising to reason, wash the stuff right out of your hair.

Re-program yourself daily until you begin to see that money is only a thing, a grubby, unimaginative piece of paper, check or plastic. You can't eat it. You can't use it like a hat to keep the rain off your head. Money is boring strings of black or red numbers.

To avoid the near occasion of money sin, stop talking about the damn stuff, stop dreaming it, living for it. Don't hang out with people who are consumed by it. Don't let them suck you into their game because all it does is to flicker your flame. Often I'll hear a money-addict shrugging off his greed by saying, "I'm not hung up on money, really. I see it just as a way of keeping score."

Score what? In the life-war game you and all of us have to play now in the United States, do you ever get to rack up such a tremendous score that you finally win? Who decides that, anyway? Who asks you: Do you have enough now? Who are you pasting up your score for?

Well, you know perfectly well who. It's the monster in you that you didn't surrender, the fanatic who'd die for the cause. It's your ego bellowing, drowning out your spirit flame until it can only whisper: Money has nothing to do whatsoever with the unique sacred person you are. That's your meaning on earth. It's your only chase that has any eternal value.Throw the paper trash into the dumpster. You can't take it with you. All that's in the pocket of your shroud is your near-death life review: the voice in you that you didn't know you knew. "When you were down there with the humans---be honest now---How much did you love?" Keep score of that, and your money sickness will eventually remit and be forgotten in your healing.

Your spirit flame burns in you to heal you. You start to heal when you make the leap into the positive electricity of courage. You're re-programming your consciousness with the knowledge that you can face, cope and handle whatever good or nasty stuff comes along. The next step toward healing is neutrality or detachment. If you get money, fine, if you don't get it, that's fine, too. Something else will turn up. The next important step upward is willingness. Here, you're reprogramming your consciousness by saying, "Okay, I'm willing myself to

144

surrender." But surrender is not passive. It's active. You have to motivate yourself daily to be willing to surrender. You have to tell yourself: I resolve to live up here in the high electricity. I resolve to heal myself by doing that.

When circumstances force you to come into contact with the money-sickness---like the flu, we're all exposed to it a thousand times a day---your motivation which you're now living tells you to remove yourself physically and emotionally---get as far away as you can---from the money-infected people, and, importantly, from the game they play.

Competition.

Competition in our society has come to mean games, not only the money-chase one, but all the spawn of it. Every kind of game you can imagine. Hitting balls with sticks, having gladiators hit each other for you, dinging computer keys and pushing your own monsters around. Games where you'd better be a winner or you're no damn good.

It hurts me to say this. I love games. I've been raised on them. I've even been proficient at a few. But now, I fear, the money-god, the big scorekeeper in the sky, has poisoned them for us. Games have become just another way of objectifying our enemy, beating the shit out of him, and the better we can beat, get to be pros, the more bucks we can make, whether actual ones or just for the insatiable bank account of our egos.

Games are supposed to be recreation. By letting go to their sheer fun, we hope to re-create ourselves. Be like children again. Become new, freed men and women for these happy moments. But lately, it doesn't seem to work out that way. Even the two nature sports that I love, hunting and fishing, have for many of us been monetized. I take a lot of people fly fishing with me. Some are big hitters from the money game in the cities. Too often when we're drifting lazily down the Green River, with moose staring at us from willows on the bank and baby mallards skittering away, my guy in the back of the boat could care less about nature's treasure. Instead, he's grimly flicking out his fly line, hitting target after target in the dark eddies. He's zinging for things. Shooting for numbers. He'll get a fish on, play it quick, dump it back in with barely a glance at the splendor of its color.

145

Re-tool and lash again. Catch another, another. We're into score-keeping here. Poor devil has brought the office with him right out into the stream. It's all he knows. He can't help it. Nature isn't worth inhaling and revering. It's simply a place where the numbers live.

I've watched city number-counters out there in the frozen dawn, beating the waters. I try to tell them the fish don't get up this early. Wait for the sun, the hatch. But they keep lashing away so they can talk about their scores that night over drinks. Sometimes these competitors want to get me into a fishing contest with them. They've got to have somebody to beat, and if it's the guy who claims to know this water, that's even a better trophy to bring home. When I tell them that I don't want to fish against them, that I enjoy it more just being there and seeing somebody else's joy, they look at me blankly.

It's even worse in the hunting field. There, unlike fish you can release and let live again, you shoot to kill and stuff dead bird bodies into your pocket. See? I got these. I shot better than you did, I'm some punkins. Up at a duck club in the California desert where I used to hunt, we had one particularly rapacious kill-counter. Whenever the canvasbacks would stream over our boats, we'd all blast out a barrage. Birds would fall. Nobody knew who hit what, but invariably, here'd be this clown shouting: "My bird! My bird!" Off he'd paddle to grab the thing before somebody else could snitch his number from him. Particularly ludicrous because after the hunt we always divided the birds equally between all of us. The meat didn't matter. He was shooting ego.

I hunt for the joy of watching my dogs work and for the blessing of being out in nature, preferably alone. It's a vertical meditation, I think---until the money-shooters crowd in and hope to tan my hide with the splendid feathers of a bird. Anymore, I feel a tinge or remorse at any bird that falls, whether from my gun or anyone else's. I love these noble creatures. Love them enough so that like the Indians, I want to beg the All to forgive me for removing one from the Whole. When I hear tales of my hunting friends, paying small fortunes to slaughter hundreds, even thousands of driven grouse, pheasant or partridge in the old hunting fields of Europe, I'm sickened at the pride with which they count their numbers.

In the way we were raised, competition says you win, I lose, or vice versa. You have to beat somebody, some object. Now, what does this do to your spirit/flame? Unless you can insulate yourself with incredible detachment, competition plunges you down into desire, anger and pride. Worse, whenever you fail to be a skilled enough competitor, you tighten up in fear. Nice guys finish last. You just weren't good enough or tough enough to step into the circle with the winners. A player addicted to the money game must win at all costs. These are life games, remember? When applying for a job at a major corporation, the personnel screeners like you best if you have in your resume excellence in some sport. It's clear what they're looking for. Somebody with the competitive killer-instinct, and at the same time a loyal team player. I know of many people who have landed good jobs just because they were good athletes.

In the entertainment business in California, tennis, in my time, was the make-break game. If you hung around the courts of the pretty people and happened to have a helluva forehand, somebody might drop a picture into your lap some day. I was once playing doubles against a famous movie star. He and the court loungers were betting a thousand dollars a game. Back then, I could usually hit a strong serve. In the midst of the game I whacked one, an ace that half-way knocked the racquet out of Star's hand. To my amazement, he roared: "Serve again! I wasn't ready!" Not ready? It was something like forty-five, in my side's favor. I'd served to him several times in the last moments. You don't play not ready in the middle of a game, but he was allowed to. Star, with a thousand bucks on it. When I served again, I was so damn mad I double-faulted. I guess he got the score he wanted.

Of all the games that money has poisoned, it seems to me that golf is the sickest. Instead of being a pleasant walk in the green with friends, it's now become a mechanized ego-war where numbers on a card become the symbols of a human's worth. The big-hitters in business and finance flock eagerly to golf because it's an extension of their life war in the office. The very hazards of beating a little ball into holes in the ground day after day are clearly akin to beating a dollar out of the bottom line. Better still, you can also put money on it here. You get a clear winner who has to get paid. Along comes some kid who's new in the executive suite. You try him on the golf course. If he hangs in skillfully for the 18, that's a boy to watch. If, however, he proves himself a duffering oaf, you look at him with an amused kind of scorn. He just doesn't have it. No comer here who can lend something to the company team.

Try this experiment. Go to your neighborhood golf course, preferably an up-scale country club. Watch the foursomes carting in after the 18th hole. Study the faces closely. Is there joy in them, any real camaraderie? Chances are, no. The guys are tense, tired. Their mumbling lips are replaying the bogey they shot on 12 and the quadruple putt on 14. They're consistently downgrading their performance, e.g., themselves and their worth as human beings. A tiny ball and a shaft of aluminum has slashed them down into the bottom of the box. And what's worse, two of the four guys are winners. Now, at the 19th hole for drinks and at the dinner party that night, they're apt to be dragging innocent bystanders stroke by dreary stroke through their glorious victory. Eyes glaze over, particularly the poor gal who is the guy's dinner partner .

We tend to forget that before the United States industrialized and a majority of people still lived on the land, they played mostly land-oriented games. They walked, trapped, hunted and fished. They raced on foot or with horses, had a few turkey shoots and dances. They rarely even went to the seashore for recreation. It hadn't yet become fashionable. But then, during the Civil War, when men were caged into prisons, one of them, Abner Doubleday, worked out a game with sticks, balls and running that became baseball. And soon, when restless, angry immigrants became caged as workers in the city factories, they couldn't very well punch their boss in the face. So they had to develop a new outlet for their anger. They could run balls, kick balls and smash into each other. Football was born. When there weren't enough city parks so that all the workers could play it, they picked helmeted gladiators to do it for them. Now they had the vicarious thrill of watching others play at caveman-like mayhem. Tribes quickly developed, neighborhood against neighborhood, city against city. The gladiators got bigger and fiercer and more violent. They became millionaires, too, and thus the N leagues were born. NFL, NL, NBA, NHL.

Don't knock it. When you're a poor man, particularly of color, being the best and most violent competitor was a springboard out of the ghetto. You had all this testerostone anger building in you. How better to let it out than by smashing a ball or puck or fist into your neighbor's face.There have been heroic stories of men lifting themselves out of poverty by their athletic feats, which often have a meaning that outlives them.

In the mysterious ways consciousness works, there's an upside to competitive games. When you set a home run record or break the 4 minute mile, what you actually do is to create a new paradigm. By your example, you have lifted everybody up, and others will soon follow into the vacuum you've filled. Jung might call it synchronicity. Random chance with meaning.

There seem to be two downsides in the exultation and monetization of games. When man stops worshipping God, he often begins worshipping his body and health. The jogging and fitness crazes come out of such thinking. They're fulfilling and probably beneficial pursuits, but again, like the "my bird" man, when they're done in ego wantingness, they become just one more war against ourselves. I've known several Ulysses-like athletes. Unable to let their ego youth go, they literally drove themselves until they blew their hearts on the tennis or squash court or the jogging track.

Again, detachment from the competitive drug is the only antidote. Go back to the fun of games and leave all the self-proving out of them. But it's tricky to do. Take bird-watching, or "birding" as the in's call it. Now what could be more lovely and spiritual than a walk in the fields, glassing the tufted tit willow or the lesser scaup? But then when the peaceful seekers get back into the tour bus, are they overjoyed by their blessed moment in nature? Some surely are, but unfortunately, more and more now seem to have come down with the number sickness. On their little scorecards, they're checking off the species they've spotted that you didn't. Beat you to it, fella. I got six white-breasted nut hatches to your measly one common house wren and one shitepoke.

The other ill wind of competion that flickers your spirit flame is the tribalism of it. You're drawing just one more circle like the religions do. We Catholics-Baptists-Fundamentalists-Jews, we, whatever, have the true faith. We're inside the circle and you guys are out. Why else do soccer matches in Europe often break up into deadly riots? The other guy's team is the enemy. Kick him out, kill him! A young cowboy in Wyoming is so addicted to his Dallas Cowboys that he and his kids not only wear all their accoutrements, but when the Cowboys lose on a given Sunday, the father plunges into black depression and can barely say a civil word to anybody for several days.

I've done it myself and suspect you have, too. How many beautiful Sunday afternoons have we spent, sitting in a soft chair, pigging out on one pro football game after another? Your wife or you pal comes in and wants to take a walk or ride a bike with you. Uh-uh. The Vikings are on the ten yard line with only a minute to go, and after they're done, the Niners are up against the Broncos to see who gets into the playoffs. Hours later when the sun has finally gone down, your gobbled sandwich is still in your throat, your burning eyes yearning for Murine, your brain stuffed with ceaseless commercials for stuff you didn't want anyway and could never afford. What did you learn? What did you gain? Certainly not the peace of the here and now. In the roaring of the crowds and the shilling of the shills, you've just killed a little more time in your war of life---watching somebody else win or lose theirs.

If we've come to see competitive games as life, and as games grow increasingly violent, then life is permitted to grow more violent, too, and be regarded as something we have to win big and cash in on.

Your spirit flame is there to heal you. Maybe after the last game is over, if you have time, you'll even look at it closer. What you're apt to see, hope you see, is compassion for yourself. You're only human. You couldn't help flickering your flame with your dollars and your ego and your games. But the flame says, Life, my friend, is not there at all. It only lives in loving your humanness, forgiving yourself and the world that puts you to so many tests.

Do that, and you no longer have to keep score.

16.

I took one final try at getting to the spirit on the religious road. It wasn't an ashram this time. It was something as mundane as a little male part in the control box of a well. It was electricity, challenging me and demanding that I have the courage at last to stop drying up the water of my soul.

Winters in California it's supposed to rain. But in January 1987 when I'd just added another fifty cows and calves, drought hit us. On parched, denuded hills the cattle moped around, thin as razorbacks and eyeing me mournfully. Wobbly, new-born calves were humped up in the cold and bleating because their mommas' teats had only dry dreams.

It was a good time to get me away from the ranch, Teddy said, and whisked me off to a married couples retreat in the nearby Santa Cruz mountains. Not necessarily my idea of a socko weekend, but I figured to assuage myself by looking down on beautiful Monterey bay, and refueling in memories of the Pacific I loved. As it turned out, the retreat house hulked in a gloomy canyon, its only vista being a damp, mossy redwood grove best suited for snails.

The curriculum was ultimate hard-line. Though we were bound to silence again, our mentors permitted us to stare at each other wordlessly during a brief cocktail. By the second night, I'd inhaled enough heavy duty religion to realize that our entire life was wrong. Our kids were raised and gone. Teddy and I were knocking around in emptiness on thousands of acres of land. And for what? For me to write books that came harder than ever and reached fewer people? Or to try to get to God, when even here on His turf I wasn't listening? No, I concluded, it was time to put my spiritual money where my mouth was.

If Teddy and I really wanted to get to God, shouldn't we chuck the world whole hog and go?

Scribbling furiously, I worked out a plan where we'd sell the ranches, sell my beloved horses and bird dogs, stop being enslaved by too many THINGS, most of which were so old they didn't work.

Then what?

Well, we'd do what the scriptures said. Give away whatever we had left. Get out like Mother Theresa and mix it up with the poor someplace where the end game was not pleasuring ourselves but helping others to stay alive. Teddy was always talking about wanting to work in the jungle villages of Central America. How much wanting time did we have left? Do it now! After the ashram experience, I cringed at another suffer-trip, but possibly we could work out a home and home arrangement. I'd go to her jungle for a few ghastly months, and in payback she'd go with me to my beach shack in Hawaii, body-surfing in the rainbows. If there was time left over, I'd finally be able to launch a magazine and film series I'd dreamed of. <u>South</u> <u>Seas.</u> Shades of my youth out in the islands fair, working with people, not animals, and hopefully helping to explore the wonders of the world's last great frontier.

After the retreat was over and we were driving home, I tried my dream on Teddy. I only had a brief shot at her. We had to stop at a body shop where my old deisel truck was being repaired. More important, Teddy was preparing a catechism lesson for the Mexican kids she'd teach that night. When I finally managed to catch her attention, she gave me her answer short and sweet. No! There would not be one more of my off the world dreams. She'd already followed me to three ranches, five houses and seven states. We were not starting all over again---she almost shrieked it---"on some damn Hawaiian island!"

At the body shop, she nudged me. "Please get out. I'm late for my children now."

"Well, dammit, at least wait to see if I can get the lousy truck started."

She did, and it did. I grudged back to the ranch alone, muttering the arguments I should have used and had been storing up all the years we'd been out on the ranches. But when I finally turned in on our lonely, dusty road, deer were staring at me in the dusk and a quail covey skittered off to roost. For an instant, I felt a familiar relief that she'd saved me from myself again.

154

The heady glow lasted until I came across the house cattleguard. Our tiny garden that had cost years of Teddy's landscaping was now milling with dozens of dumb beasts. My starving cow herd had broken jail, ripped down fences and were grubbing up the only green plants this side of Hawaii. I jumped out of the truck and began shooing them out. I was stepping in fresh cow plops, then flinging rocks. A few cattle would leave but other more starved ones would rush in. You can rarely move cows on foot, least of all in the dark. I tried chasing them in the truck but couldn't get very far without tearing up Teddy's garden even worse. In fury, I raced down to the ranch shop where J.D. our foreman had left our four wheeler Honda bike. Turned the key. The battery was stone cold dead.Where was J.D. to help me start it? Well, I knew where. This redoubtable kid who'd been giving us tender loving care for years was off catching the surf in Hawaii---vacation from the ranch and the dreams.

Bleakly, I stalked into the house. It was cold and dark. We had no central heat. Teddy was saving money by having us cut the over-abundance of oaks that dotted our hills. I tried to fire up the wood stove which any Mexican girl of four can do instantly, but my version, wisping weakly on dead ashes, would take hours to heat up the house. So instead, I'd warm up with a good hot bath. I leaned over the tub, opened the faucet. GLOOP.

Bone dry. The pipes were frozen. In fact, the entire Rube Goldberg water system of the ranch was frozen in the harshest cold snap my neighbor could remember since "the miserable bugger in '32." I raced around much of the night, cobbling up fences as best I could and scooping water out of the backs of the toilets to give my bird dogs a drink. When Teddy finally came home from spreading the faith to her kids, she groaned at the sea of cow manure and ravaged plants. But there was no time to mourn. Her father had had a mild stroke. Early the next day, she flew off to Memphis to be with him. As I hugged her goodbye, she said, "I hope you can get everything fixed. And stop being so cranky about it. This is our life, darling. Love it, please…"

Who's cranky? Who's got a book to write instead of hammering on broken stuff and chasing dumb beasts around? About then, loyal J.D. phoned from Hawaii, giving me some long distance alchemy about how to fix the house water tank pump and check three miles of plastic piping for possible leaks. He'd barely hung up before my TV dish blipped to dead gray screen---now I was really off the world. Then the phone went out. Somebody up the line had tried to dig up his frozen pipes with a backhoe and chopped the cable. As a last straw, our old faithful river well that watered the entire ranch chose this convenient moment to give up its ghost. We were now bone dry, up the creek in a big lead boat.

Okay, get help. But where? It was Martin Luther King Day. Every neighbor I tried was "off visitin' family" far away. All known mechanics were on long weekends. Even the pump wizards who'd helped us in the past were too busy repairing major agricultural damage to worry about a few pissant cows way back in the hills.

The big nasty ball was squarely in my court. It would be me or nobody.

So down I went three miles to the river and stared at the gray control box on the well. Inside this monster were 220 volts, waiting to fry the amateur who messed with it. Even my brave ranch neighbors wouldn't touch the thing with a pole. The box was plastered with all sorts of warning signs, shut this off before you did that. But my electrical knowledge barely allows me to change a light bulb let alone shut what and do what? The juice was clearly humming inside the box and not one sign or lever showed me how to shut the damn thing off.

I shuddered at the memory of my last attempt at solving a mechanical problem.

On a dark, rainy night in 1945, we were about to fly our general, Roy S. Geiger USMC, out of Okinawa. The battle was over. He'd declared the island secure. But we had a problem the grizzled old aviator didn't know about. The new aircraft we'd brought him from Pearl Harbor was siphoning ten gallons of gas an hour out of its cabin tanks. With all the water we had to cross, we needed every drop. In some stroke of my new-found mechanical genius, I told the crew chief to cut off the gas tank vent lines so that they were flush with the skin of the fuselage, as they had been on our old plane which didn't siphon.

Fine, as far as it went. An hour later we were banging through storm out of Okinawa with the cockpit smelling like a Texaco station. When we finally pulled up the floorboards to find what the trouble was, the entire belly of the plane was sloshing with explosive aviation gas four inches deep. Well, now, who tells the General? Me. I ran into the cabin with life jackets for him and his staff and begged him to douse his cigar. We limped on back to Okinawa with our fingers in our ears, waiting for the bomb to go off. Until now, it's never been revealed how close I came to blowing up some of the most valuable Marines in the Pacific, present company excluded!

So, decades later, down by the riverside, I scowled at my latest booby trap. the gray control box and said aloud, "By God, I am going to do this! Right this time, please God."

I opened the box, contrary to the warnings. A tiny metal male part was staring at me. If I had the courage to twist this thing, wouldn't it somehow make the pump deep in the well come to life? My fingers trembled. The juice had to be on in the box. Was the male part hot, too? Wiser men wouldn't touch it with a pole? What about my own pole? In abject cowardice, I was like my pointer dog, rustling through the grass to find a scrap of wood or anything non-conductive. It looked ridiculous, it *was* ridiculous, a grown man rooting around as if "root hog or die."

Finally, my fingers touched wood. Two pieces, old axe handles long abandoned by some pioneer before us, and probably before electricity. I seized them, and as carefully as a brain surgeon, clamped them against the male part. Foiled again! The part had some metal frammis on the widget below it that had to be raised before the cursed thing would turn. Then I was back in the dead grass again, rooting up tiny little sticks, stones and detritus of the ages. I stuffed them below the widget, held up the frammis long enough to seize the male part again and twist it.

No shock. I was still on my feet, the pump coming on in a glorious humm, and water beginning to shower out of the vent pipe. We were back in the world, back to life! Hail Holy Queen!

When J.D. finally returned from the islands fair, he glowered at me. "What in hell did you do in the power box, Big O? It's all filled up with little sticks like a mouse was in there."

I said it was a matter of the danger, and he snorted, "What danger? That thing is as safe as a church!"

Maybe it was only perilous to a mouse, who didn't know a male part from a soul.

All I knew was, for my incessant dreams of easier, greater glory beyond, I could never let go of this life. Teddy was right. Be who I was, where I was. Running off to some new place had nothing at all to do with happiness. No, I had to keep writing the hard way and pasturing dumb beasts who ate the plants and pooped on the poetry. Kind of a prayer, and perhaps realizing at last that it's not because I want to do it or must, but because, in some timorous balancing act of caring and not caring, I think it's what God wants me to do. And has tried, with bounteous patience, to keep me at it all these years.

17

"You are the maker of the dream," Mark Twain said.

When you motivate yourself to live as much as possible in the higher levels of consciousness, you not only have an excellent chance of creating the life you've imaged, but more important, you can heal yourself on the journey.

My great aunt Nora knew how to do it.

This tall, henna-rinsed lady was my grandfather Will's sister, and like him, an immigrant from Mayo, the poorest county in Ireland. In the tradition of the Irish clan, she lived with us in our house from the time I was born through all the years until my own children were raised. Whether it was her natural peasant simplicity or her faith, Nora knew how to let go and let God make the dream of her life come true.

When one of my cousins asked her, "Aunt Nora, I've heard that your mother, Bridget Fahey, was the strongest woman in Mayo, and could lift a hundred pound grain sack onto her head," Nora drew herself up archly, her blue eyes blazing. "Young man," she said, "my mother never lifted anything heavier than a tea cup."

Years later, when Will took Nora back to Mayo with him, they stood together out on the lonely moor of Carney's Field. They were staring at the same tiny, thatch-roofed cottage that Teddy and I saw. "But Will," Nora said hesitantly, "where is our big house?"

He smiled. "That's it, Nora. That's all it ever was."

In Nora's dream, she'd created a new, grand identity. Her journey hadn't been easy. As a young girl, she'd come from the gentle, green land of Ireland, to be dumped down into noisy, brawling Chicago. In terror, she'd had to flee the great fire, clinging in a rowboat to what few possessions she had. A few years later, trying to elope with a man her brothers disapproved of, her lover's carriage overturned. Nora was thrown out and suffered internal injuries. She had to have a hysterectomy, surely a perilous operation in the 1880's. She developed angina, crippling her in painful spasms for the rest of her life.

But Nora resolved to go beyond her body. Her dream was to be a painter and a world traveler. Thanks to her pluck and her brother, Will's support, she managed to do both. She visited places like Zanzibar, Zululand and Tristan de Cunha before most people even knew where they were. When my brother Bill and I were young, Nora fascinated us with her tales of adventure. She'd read us stories by the hour, or she'd dress up in outrageous costumes and delight us with her skits of the tinkers and leprechauns from the Other Side.

In later years, she wintered at the Arizona Biltmore Hotel in Phoenix. She was the first guest to come there, and had a room of her own that was never rented out, filled as it was with her paints and desert landscapes. After 40 years, the Biltmore gave her a silver loving cup. She was the grande dame of the place, dressing for dinner every night, tall and erect, sweeping down the red-flowered stairway with an ermine cape swirled over her shoulders.

What a long way she'd come from the lonely moor of Carney's Field. And the secret of her dream, I think, was her joy of life. She'd wiped out the past. When I'd try to lure her into talking about the old days in Mayo, she'd flick them away with a toss of her head, as if there never had been an Other Side or the Big House that wasn't. She'd programmed herself to live in the high, healing emotions. Always the optimist, she refused to wear black or go to funerals. She wouldn't even read the Irish Sport Page, which was what we called the obituaries. As her incredible years of good health spooled on, she wouldn't let herself dwell on sickness or death. When oldsters at the Biltmore would try to tell her about their latest illness or operation, Nora would smile and make a graceful exit. Though her own angina was a constant problem, she never mentioned it, and wouldn't answer if you asked her how she felt. She'd programmed herself to feel well, and be grateful for each blessed day God gave her.

Nora lived in our house for 50 years. Imagine the poor bride of today with her husband's aunt down the hall in her own room for a half century. Nora shone her light on all of us and we treasured her. When she was 96, she was still gamely out on our lawn, chipping approach shots to an imaginary green. At 97, she happened to break her foot. Mother took her to the hospital. The young doctor was amazed at the x-rays. "Miss Carney," he said, "these are incredible bones. Would you mind telling me how old you are."

Nora drew herself up. "You're the doctor, lad. You tell me."

What he did tell her was to wear the corrective shoe he'd prescribed. In the first snows of Christmas, Nora flung the ugly thing away. She winced into her smart pumps and pegged around shopping at Marshall Field's.

When she was 98, still with all her faculties and joy of life, she came down for breakfast one morning and told Mother that she'd seen "the bird at the window." Mother, Irish herself, knew what the old country saying meant. The bird was there to take a soul.

"I won't have the Lord seeing me in such a mess," Nora said, and asked Mother to take her to the hairdresser. That night, with a new permanent, henna rinse, and a Biltmore evening gown, she had dinner with my mother and father. Then she went up to her room, lay down with her rosary, and sometime before dawn, she went with the bird.

Let her life go. I still marvel at the majesty and peace of her surrender.

How do we do it today, you and I?

What Nora's life seems to mean is that if you live your dream, care tremendously about giving it your all, leaping to the courage of the high emotions, then indeed you've managed to live in havingness. You have everything you've ever needed. When your time is done, you've already had your reward. You can not care to hold onto it, knowing in your faith that your spirit flame burns eternally, in some miraculous ways that you don't yet know that you know.

If Nora had lived her love, joy and peace so well, wasn't she believing that she would continue to have exactly that, wherever she would go from here?

In your world and mine today, such detachment is not easy to come by. We live in a society that's hung up on body and death. We don't want to let our human container go because, if we don't have faith in the wonders of our spirit, we believe that our bodies are all we have. It all ends in the grave.

"You are not your body," David Hawkins observes. "You are your spirit. Your body is really not much more than a little karmic wind-up toy. It's perfectly capable of taking care of itself better than you can."

But you have to give it a chance.

How? Do as Nora did. Reject negative thoughts and emotions. Live as much as possible in the positive, healing ones

If we can cure ourselves in our heads, why don't we do it more often? I suspect there are three reasons.

---We don't believe enough in the spirit to trust the power it can give us.

---even if we do believe in it, we haven't motivated ourselves enough to keep plugging away at mental healing on a daily or even hourly basis. We just don't want to take the time to practice something so esoteric.

---we have been brainwashed by the massive medical industry to believe that science and technology are the only avenues to healing. We allow ourselves to become their passive victims, instead of leaping to courage and taking command of our own health.

Like many of our other systems, American medicine still operates under the parts-thinking of Newton and Bacon. It is based on doing, not being, and has steadfastly refused to consider that our doing joined with our being is the only way we can successfully treat the whole, non-dualistic human that we are.

U.S. medicine is a triumph of technology. Decades of research and brilliant innovations have evolved space-age techniques by which doctors can identify the broken part and treat it or replace it. Medicine imitates the ancient production line, spooling out given quotas of human product, packaged and marketed by physicians or drug companies.

But gradually, change is coming. Younger doctors particularly are breaking away from the old traditions and treating their patients holistically. Some, like Harvard-trained

Andrew Weil recognize that although American medicine is the best in the world for treating traumas, how do we cope with the mental causes of illness? What are the effects of spirit on our bodies? What about herbs and placebos? Are we reaching a point where we can rise above the parts-thinking and begin treating the whole? Why do we get sick in the first place? And more than treating the illness after it's happened, why not get in there first? Activate the patient's spirit to heal itself *before* the crisis occurs.

The roadblock to such pioneering vision is partly stolid, stubborn medical tradition, and partly, the industrializing of health. If people are sick, they're going to pay dearly to get healed. This is when fear enters the game. We can be made afraid of a certain disease or ailment. In the media, medical scare stories or longed-for cures drench us daily. Our spirit, that innocent naïve child, is sucking it all in. If you're living down in the low emotions, what better way to heap guilt, fear or hate on yourself than to seize on some dreaded disease you might just have. Spirit acts on your emotional response and flashes a signal to your body to act out what you've presented.

Nora's answer was simply to walk away from hearing that stuff. Don't pop the fear loop into your computer.

Lately, two terrifying threats seem to be sweeping across our society. Suppose you got breast cancer or prostate cancer? In a culture that still has trouble coping with its sexuality, what a horrible blow this must be to the ego. Your very-life force is on the line here

But there's another side of the story we don't hear about. "When I was in medical school at Columbia right after World War II," says David Hawkins, "we rarely if ever saw breast cancer, and nobody thought much about the prostate, either."

What irony that these are the most prevalent and increasing forms of cancers. What does the trend tell us? Why now have the conditions reached epidemic proportions? Could it be the fear that's been attached to them, and pumped into our spirit? Only the rare individual seems able to counteract the negative program by installing a positive one, canceling it repeatedly by telling ourselves that we're not subject to such conditions.

Regarding another terrible fear, the dread of tobacco,

163

Hawkins performs a dramatic experiment. Using the technique of kinesiology, testing the body's response to noxious substances, he'll have a young woman hold against her navel a package containing a pack of a name-brand cigarette. Immediately, her immune system is stressed. Her muscles go weak. Her spirit, reporting what her body told it, says "bad stuff!"

Then Hawkins gives her another package. She holds it against her navel, which seems to be the seat of the body's feeling reaction. When her body responds, the immune system doesn't protest. Her muscles go strong.

Then Hawkins opens the package and pours small brown flakes into his hand. They're tobacco---but here's the surprise---this tobacco is organically grown. Tobacco, he says, is just a neutral plant, harmless. The problem with growing it commercially is that insects devour about half the crop. A lot of money is at stake here, so, back in the early 1950's, the cigarette companies began using a powerful pesticide to kill the bugs. That's the poison in cigarettes. The bugs die and so do the people.

Thus, a fear monster emerged. Indeed, tobacco would surely kill when it was loaded with poison, so we must wipe it out. An anti-smoking industry was created, billions of dollars involved and massive government intrusion. "The irony of it," Hawkins says, "the government could simply order the tobacco growers to raise an organic crop. Sure, the companies would lose half of their leaves, but people could still smoke without harm to themselves because pure, organic tobacco is benign. If we did that, all the dollars spent and the sound and futy of tobacco prohibition would be unnecessary."

An even sillier example of our anti-smoking crusade came to light when Hawkins was co-authoring *Ortho-molecular Psychiatry* with his friend Linus Pauling. The controversial Nobelist attracted great attention by his research on what he claimed were the wonders of Vitamin C. "Linus believed," Hawkins says, "and proved to his own satisfaction that the effects of the tobacco pesticide could be counteracted and neutralized by a certain large daily dose of vitamin C. That would have been another alternative for the embattled smoker, but it was too late by then. The anti-smoking industry was impossible to fight. Too many people and bureaucracies depended on it for a living."

If fear, however induced, is a threat to your health, if it flickers the flame of your spirit, how do you counteract it?

Again, the answer seems to lie in avoiding it. Of course, physically, you try to distance yourself from fear thoughts or the people who espouse them. But on a higher level of consciousness, where you've motivated yourself to live as much as possible, you begin to develop an *awareness* about what thoughts you're going to allow to enter your head. You begin getting damn choosy about junk food for the brain. When a fear thought starts whirling toward you, you laugh at it---that's okay for somebody else but it's not mine---and you fling it back like a boomerang to whoever threw it at you.

The more awareness you can focus on your incoming thoughts, the less power they have over you. You are literally spiking a lie before it starts running its tape. Once you set up such a pattern, your spirit seems to "get it," and becomes a willing, clever ally in helping you to shoot down the noxious stuff.

For the terrified souls who can't rise above their medical fears, David Hawkins has coined a name: "Bubble People." These individuals try to live in a hermetically-sealed sanitized dome where nothing can harm them. If they walk into a room and sniff, they cry out, "Somebody has smoked in here!" They flee. Or, they refuse to enter a certain building lest they get a whiff of asbestos from the insulation, or mold or lint. Name it. They're afraid of everything. One group of Bubble People were colleagues of Hawkins. When they'd meet weekly for a seminar, Hawkins would gulp down the greasy chicken and french fries, but not the doctors. They sat at a separate table, their lunches in brown paper bags. They ate grains organically grown in Iran, pure yogurt from Yugoslavia, fruit and nuts from other far off lands, not a horrid chemical in the lot. Did their Bubble People diet improve their health? "I can't ask them," Hawkins says, "they're all dead."

Teaching yourself to develop your awareness seems to work best when you make it part of a daily meditative practice. Now, everyone has his or her own ways of touching the spirit. The masters have been doing it for centuries. Great books have been written about it. The search for soul has now become a publishing industry, so many of us are out there looking. In light of all the professionals in the field, I hesitate to describe my own gropings because they're such homespun techniques.

On a perfect day---and I have damn few of them because I'm still driving with my spiritual learners' permit---I try to greet my wake-up call by inserting two thoughts into my consciousness computer. *Love yourself and be happy.* There are no prayers attached to this, just two human commands from my control tower. What I'm trying to program against may be genetic. Unlike Nora, many Irish allow themselves to live in a kind of melancholy, a sunless mist weeping over the moors, and are quick to hate themselves when they lose their way in it. So I find that the self-loving, happy program not only cuts the gloom but does wonders to light up the new day. (And sure, after an hour or so when the first mundane challenge presents itself, you're apt to lapse back into old downer mode, but at least now you know what you're doing and it doesn't have such power over you.)

Forgetting and blowing it is perfectly human, so you build into your program an automatic screen-saver: compassion for self. Let your weakness go. Forgive it. Then you reinforce it by taking the next step which in our case begins in the bathroom.

On a normal day, Teddy is already there, about ten laps ahead of me in her mind/body work. She's a big exerciser. Long before I can haul myself out of bed, she's planted herself on her yoga mat and is well into a ballet-like routine of stretches and pulls that have managed to keep her lithe and supple well into her seventies. She's physically tough as well.

Several years ago at the ranch, she was out checking the cattle with our granddaughter, Nora. It was a leisurely ride. Teddy has cowboyed for four decades on the ranches. She's walked away from her share of falls, too, but none like this one. In the midst of a slow canter, her stirrup buckle crystallized and broke. She was riding a tall, reliable cow horse, but he has a rough canter, and when she lost her balance, she pitched off and splatted onto hard ground without getting a hand under her. What Nora saw in horror was her grandmother with her arm wrapped around her neck like a noodle. The local doctor said it was the worst break he'd ever seen, seventeen fractures that took an equal number of pins and plates to put back together. The orthopedic surgeon doubted that she's ever regain full use of her arm. He prescribed extensive therapy. When Teddy is given a medical order---her own grandfather, Willis Campbell was a pioneer orthopedic surgeon in Memphis---she responds like a fire horse at the bell.

Back then, we had an old Mexican woman, Herminia, housekeeping for us. Illiterate, unable to speak English, she was cunning, manipulative and devoted to us. Teddy was determined to teach Herminia to meditate. While Teddy's meditation would usually drift off into mundane head noise, Herminia reported soaring into an angelic state of silent blankness where, more than once, *El Senor Jesu Christo* himself appeared. When the broken arm happened, Herminia took it as a challenge and opened up with her heavy artillery. Three times a day, she'd lay Teddy down on our dining room table, both of them praying, Teddy wailing in pain as Herminia's strong fingers would be kneading her arm like tortilla dough. Something must have been going on. Gradually, Teddy began feeling her muscles come back to life. Within several months, she had regained full use of her arm.

What did it? High voltage prayer, or muscle-work, or both? *Quien sabe*? Herminia always seemed to *know* it would heal, and maybe it's the knowing that makes it happen.

Now, on my own morning routine, when I join Teddy in the bathroom, my creaky body is groaning from sleep. I can feel every rusty joint and I dread putting them down on the floor and grinding them.

But Teddy refuses to let me off so easy, and I thank her for that---eventually. At first, I feel like I'm back in the Marine Corps being punished with calesthentics. Body worship. The hell with body. I want to be into consciousness, the control tower that runs my karmic windup toy.

Well, after all the push and pull and some yogic breathing

thrown in for good measure, it does seem that the mind becomes dulled or bored enough to let go of the problems of the day. At this point, I lie face down in the butterfly yoga position, the abject surrender pose, knees bent, head on the mat and arms stretched as far as I can get them above my shoulders.

Then, in my amateurish, non-monkish words, I pray for the Holy Spirit to come into me and let me live this day as much as I can in the high healing levels of love, joy and peace.

Kindness. I want to project out kindness to the world. Lifting my hands with the palms out, I try to transmit this thought, first to humanity in general, and then, turning my palms inward, projecting kindness to myself. The forgiveness of surrender.

Thy will be done, not mine anymore.

All done, that ought to do it. But not quite. I dress and go out and kneel at Teddy's predieux on which she's draped all sorts of crucifixes and photos of hollow-eyed, big bellied children starving in various parts of the world. But all I'm looking at in this moment is my K-Mart white candle. I kneel there and light it. The flame is bright and full. I stare at it, resolving to keep it that way, this day. Get rid of any fears, doubts or ego games that just make it flicker and go weak.

Because the idea is, I want to offer up the brightest flame I can to the life force that loves me and gave me life. Gratitude. Thanks for my havingness.

At that, I blow out the candle, go into the kitchen and switch on the endless loop of Dixieland delivered by my satellite dish. There's news available too, but I rarely turn it on. The hell with news. I've been in that business and I know it's all negative. They have to keep it that way to keep you tuning in and seeing what worse things can happen to you. But I've already had the best, the flip side, and lazily blissed, I dawdle over breakfast until conscience makes me rejoin the chase of the new day.

Does such a primitive system work? I really don't know. As just a plain civilian, I still have bad days and good days like everyone else, I suppose. But slowly, over the years, I've come to believe that some sort of meditative practice does sharpen your awareness about what's hurting you and snaps you back into working on your demons and casting them out.

168

Hawkins and the other consciousness pioneers are basically talking about electrical energy. Your electricity is running your computer and you and every part of you right down to your thoughts and prayers. If you have this wondrous electricity at your disposal, the challenge seems it to be learning how to focus it best. You certainly don't want to burn yourself up with it as if you were incinerating a wood tick in the flame of a match. You want to beam that electric power out onto your own problems and to others with theirs and eventually to all of humankind.

Psychologists, holistic physicians and spiritual masters are making amazing discoveries about prayer. It appears to be an electrical energy beamed out into the overlapping holograms of the collective consciousness. If every thought and action ever performed by humans is stored here eternally, then prayer is no exception. Its electricity is focused on some thing or some one. We may not understand how radio waves or radar work, but we accept their power. Prayer seems to be a similar energy.

If it isn't, then why will one laboratory tray of bean sprouts flourish when they've been actively prayed for, and a nearby tray of sprouts will barely stay alive without prayer? When salt water is poured over both trays, the prayed-for sprouts pull through, the non-prayed for wither and die. As a further example, in several control studies in hospitals, certain heart patients were prayed for by people who not only didn't know them but were miles away physically. Those patients improved to a much greater degree than did the ones who weren't prayed for. Even spookier, none of the patients knew they were being prayed for. Thus, there couldn't have been a placebo effect.

Normally, in prayer, you're petitioning for something good to happen to you or to someone else. But according to Larry Dossey, M.D. who's done extensive research on the subject, prayer's energy seems most effective when you abandon any goal for it. You are not asking for this or that to happen. You are simply praying that Thy Will Be Done. Praying to accept it, whatever it is. Prayer in this humble form is truly the power, the victory, of surrender.

Another electricity that our spirit provides us is called imaging. Say you have a physical ailment, anything from a stiff neck to some stricken organ. Pioneer physicians like the Simontons teach their patients how to focus on the ailing organ. Using your eyes like lasers, you turn the beams inward to illuminate your problem organ. In the stiff neck, it's your vertebrae and the muscles knotted around them. You burn your eyes inside your own skeleton and see the ailing part, how the bones look, how the muscles work. What I try to do is image the gentle white fingers of the life force or the Holy Spirit stroking the inflammation out of those muscles and re-aligining the twisted bones. We've all seen enough medical charts to have some idea what our insides look like. Now, in visualizing them, we seem to be beaming an electrical energy into them. In a sort of mental diathermy treatment, we're literally stroking them, loving them and urging them to heal. Sometimes it happens immediately. Something, some stress-knotted muscle, seems to let go. In other conditions, sometimes it takes weeks or even years of daily energy healing before the suffering alleviates.

But the positive part is, you've made the leap to courage. Instead of becoming the victim of your illness and turning it over to somebody else to treat, you have taken the responsibility yourself to focus your energy, and to let go and let God, get your ego self out of the way enough so that a cure can present itself. Maybe it will, maybe it won't, but as T.S. Eliot put it: "There is neither win nor loss. Ours is only the trying."

The salutary thing about your trying is that you've risen up from courage to neutrality/detachment, then to acceptance, then to reason, and finally to the love, joy and peace of surrender. If you are to heal, it will only be here.

Mark Twain's vision of consciousness---"You are the maker of the dream"---may well be hinting at the other great source of our healing power: our own dream life. Dreams seem to be c-mails from our consciousness, giving us a gentle nudge here or a wild panic there when we've lost our way. Our dreams try to put us back on track. Jungians consider them major correctives for the spirit.

Psychic experts like Ingo Swann believe dreams are vital to our healing. The best way to do it, he says, is to reconnect with our right brains. Dreams live there, but they seem at first glance so childish or bizzare that they're embarrassed about surfacing or waking us up in a cold sweat. Therefore, Swann advises us to encourage our own dreams. Put our analytical, ego/doing left brain on hold. Shove it aside. Let the right brain of being speak to us.

The problem is, the right brain really doesn't care for words. It thinks and acts out in pictures. When you wake up after a dream, your first instinct is to write it down---and it's better to write it than to lose it. But better still, Swann says, is to draw or even paint your dream. Now you're into the visual language your right brain comprehends. So, draw it, paint it, contemplate the weird design of it, and vital nuggets of healing information are likely to emerge.

The more you tell your right brain that you're delighted it's visiting you, and show your delight by describing it in the pictures you both can understand, then the more confidence the silly little right brain kid gets. It's as if it says to itself, "Hey, this is a nice, friendly grownup. I'm going to come back and visit him every time he needs me."

After years of trying to get myself out of the bottom of the box, I've now accumulated watercolor pads filled with icons of my dreams. Almost unfailingly, when I date them against real events or hangups I was experiencing at a certain time, those dreams are like neon signs, flashing and directing me how to get back onto the freeway. Sometimes I follow their advice, and sometimes I'm not evolved enough to process their messages. But when the little guy doesn't come to visit, or comes and I don't draw him, I miss him.

As the wonders of your spirit become more and more known to you, new, puzzling vistas begin to appear. In my own case, I found myself saying, "Look, if this thing works, if I can heal myself with it, let's suppose that you and many others can do the same. Isn't it possible that our mutual slow, painful rising toward the top of the box will have a ripple effect throughout our society? Tolstoy wrote that you can't change humanity until you change yourself. But if we *are* changing, isn't our personal enlightenment eventually going to bring major changes to our systems of living and governing ourselves?

Take the wars, cataclysms and plagues of which Thomas Merton spoke. What about our life-war today in America? If the majority of us are living in the low end emotions, aren't we shaping our systems by the our same aberrant emotional responses? Shame, fear, desire, anger and pride are torturing us almost daily, keeping us trapped in darkness. By using left brain force---our doing without our being---to solve our problems, aren't we dooming our structures to fail?

But if we *are* changing, what's our brave new world going to look like? Can we focus the power of our spirit on the problems of the day? By reconceptualizing how we look at them, can we begin to envision a future that we already know but don't yet know we know? In it, in our surrender to it, will we be able to see more clearly the true meaning of our lives?

At that point in my own struggle to rise out of the bottom of my box, I longed to learn more about the spirit electricity that runs us.

What caused the mysterious synchronicity that struck me when I had my heart problem? Why else would I have stumbled onto the miracle of spirit? I didn't ask to get sick and I didn't ask to get well. I must have let go and let God. It just happened, as it did when my old novel blew up in the war and Teddy dropped into my life.

Why? Had I risen into a different energy field?

There was only one person who might give me an answer. I said to Teddy, "We've got to go to the horse's mouth. Meet David Hawkins face to face. He's the guy who started it."

All I had of a man named David Hawkins was a fax number buried in the text of his <u>Power vs Force.</u> It had a 602 area code. I'd hoped to speak to him in person but the fax-tone was all I could get. So instead, I dashed off a quick fax, telling him what his book had done for me, and hoping he could spare a little time so that Teddy and I could interview him.

That night, he called back. He sounded tired but amused. "You mention books, films and so forth. You must be an actual writer then?"

Not in his league, I said. I never could have written <u>Power vs Force.</u>

"It's very obscure. Most people don't get it." He sighed. "Okay. I can clear you some time." He mumbled a little, checking his calendar. We settled on two days the following week. I asked how to find him, and he said it was easy. Go to Prescott, Arizona, go west from there, hit a certain canyon with red rocks and pinion pines in it. Take a right on a dirt road, then turn in when you see the scarecrow.

"Scarecrow?"

"A little fellow I made. He's wearing my boots and pants. I did two of 'em, one has fallen down, but the other is still holding my sign." He laughed. "Rattlebone Ranch. That's what we are out here, old bones rattling around in a sack. Come about eight in the morning. We'll take the day or two."

What we were going to take, I discovered, was a trip off the world into a wonderland I couldn't believe existed. As Dorothy said to her dog in the <u>Wizard of Oz</u>, "Toto, I've a feeling we're not in Kansas anymore."

We weren't, from that day on.

18.

On a morning in May, under a copper hot Arizona sky, Teddy and I turned in at the scarecrow and arrived at the Rattlebone Ranch. I shut off the engine and looked at her in dismay. He lives *here*?

Not that I'd expected a fancied Scottsdale Spanish house or a landscaped patio with a kidney shaped pool, but this place was barely distinguishable from the scraggly mesquite trees that screened it. A few dark wooden buildings were scattered around on the tawny rocky sand. A rent-a-wreck type pickup hulked in the shade. Gravel paths, hazily marked by desert plants, wandered off to no apparent destination. In the shadows of a brush pile, I spotted the lumpy gray shirt and blue jeans of the fallen scarecrow.

"Well," Teddy said, "he does seem to live quite simply,"

"You mean, if he's here at all. Where the devil would he be?"

I got out of the car and called tentatively: "Doctor Hawkins?" No answer. Then louder. "Hello! Anybody home?"

Silence, whispering on a hot desert breeze. " As the Mexicans say, we were "*abandanados*," wandering around the compound. Brushing through the naggy mesquite thorns, we tried one door and discovered a chicken house. I hallooed again, "Doctor Hawkins…?"

Below, in a small green pasture, a horse nickered faintly, or was it the bray of a jackass?

My face burned, my gut tightened. I'd put such tremendous faith in this man, literally bet my life on him---and now, not even to find him? Where was the guy who had been the leading psychiatrist in America at one time? Or why the glowing testimonials on his book: Lee Iacocca, Sam Walton, Mikhail Gorbachev, Mother Teresa telling him: "You spread joy, love and compassion. The fruit of these is peace, as you know."

What in the world would have led him to a lonely ridge of

mesquite in the high Arizona desert?

"You must be Teddy and Otis," a voice said. We whirled. An attractive young blonde woman in blue jeans had creaked open a wooden gate. Behind her was a double-wide trailer I hadn't noticed before. "Doc has just finished his breakfast. He eats hardly anything and I'm cross with him about that. He's waiting for you, though. Please come in."

We walked under a ramada, thankful for the shade. Hanging on the walls was an impressive array of tools and several bridles. Work benches and power saws were beside them. "I wish our shop at the ranch looked so neat," Teddy said. Angie, the young woman, drifted by us to the screen door. "Well, here they are, Doc."

David Hawkins welcomed us in. He was pleasant, not particularly verbal. He held Teddy's hands and looked at her intently for a moment, clearly a man who appreciates women. But he didn't fit what I'd expected. He certainly wasn't charismatic, no hot eyes or commanding voice. Soft-spoken to the point of shyness, he's slightly built, middle height, several inches shorter than me. He was wearing old cowboy boots, a tan shirt and blue jeans that had had some mileage. Hippie style, his grayish hair was in a ponytail. "Oh, sure," he said, "when I'm doing tapes for medical audiences, I get a haircut and give it the full treatment with suit and tie. They seem to want that, but not here, hmm?" His eyes had a twinkle and there were a lot of "hmm's" when he spoke.

We wandered around the trailer. It was a simple place, a few armchairs and sofas. His office was an adjoining alcove crammed with books. He didn't have air-conditioning. A swamp cooler fan was thrumming on top of the trailer. The day was already getting hot. Several house cats were slinking around. Hawkins would call, "here, Kitty," and dabbled with petting and feeding them. Angie was concerned that he was working too hard. She'd say, "Doc, you're not getting tired, are you?" He'd shake his head. Apparently he had a seven day a week practice. He was the only psychiatrist for miles around, and as an M.D. the only one who could also write prescriptions. His main work was with abused girls, predominantly Native American, in a

176

clinic an hour and a half away in Prescott. He also conducted consciousness seminars at Phoenix hospitals, and at nights worked with a Navajo AA group that he advised.

Teddy said, "I've brought us some sandwiches for lunch."

He shrugged. "I don't eat much. Sometimes I go days without food, but it's nice. Thank you."

We put the lunches in the refrigerator. Then Angie fussed around in case we'd want a soft drink or something. We didn't, but Teddy brewed up her traditional tea. During the small talk, Hawkins said quietly as if to no one, "I think I'm going into another state. I have that feeling. Hmm?"

I didn't get it. Another state? Was he talking about going to California or whatever else adjoined Arizona? He smiled. "Blissing out. I get spells of it from time to time. Go into pure consciousness. Once, up in Boston, I lived for months that way. I'd lost the self completely. Then one day I happened to walk by the mirror and saw this strange face. It scared hell out of me. Who was it? I ran out into the street."

I groped. "You mean this was sort of a---transcendent state?"

"Yes, of course. When I came back into the world I didn't know who was running for President or even about Princess Di. All gone." He sighed. "But you do serve a purpose. You just have to come back and learn all over again. You have to give the other up, and well, more or less 'pass' in society."

"Oh." I blinked and looked at Teddy.

At that moment, it dawned on me. This man we were talking to was unlike any we'd ever known. He didn't think the way we did. He wasn't even in our space. He was a presence. His responses were off-putting, as if he were speaking a different language. You never knew whether he was being quirky, funny, ruthlessly honest or just overwhelmingly kind. His humility was unnerving. The practicalities of our sort of life, or indeed of life itself, seemed irrelevant to him.

How did he get that way, I wondered? How did he reach such a state of detachment and enlightenment? I'd come here looking for answers to my own gropings for spirit. I'd even hoped that I could translate David Hawkins' wisdom and spread it to others. But now I realized that the challenge was almost

177

insurmountable. I simply didn't have the mental equipment to cope with him, let alone to communicate his thoughts to others.

By then, we'd gone back into the living room of the trailer. I was nervously fingering my pipe, desperately needing a brain fix. "Go ahead," Hawkins said. "See that stuff?" He pointed to large brown leaves draped in the kitchen. "I grow my own plants when the weather's right, or if not my daughter sends some to me from Virginia. All organic. Here," he passed me a small tin, "try it."

We both lit up the first of what were going to be a lot of pipes that day. After Teddy's tape recorder refused to work, Hawkins suggested: "We ought to video this, hmm? They brought me a camera but I'm not sure I can work the damn thing." He began fussing with the camera which Angie had set up on a tripod. None of us could figure it out. Finally, Hawkins summoned a young man, I assumed from one of the mysterious outbuildings, and he got us on line. I stared at the little green light, not a bit sure I could process what was coming up next. Hawkins grinned and turned to Teddy. "You said you had some questions. Shoot."

Teddy had never looked prettier, her knees tight together in her white skirt, a Mexican cotton blouse and a large turquoise crucifix dangling from a leather thong around her neck. She was sitting bolt erect, as if she were an earnest little southern girl, back again in Sunday school. On her knees was a large notebook filled with pages of questions she'd copiously recorded out of Power vs Force.

She was nervous, her voice was tight. "I have so many things, Doctor, more than you want, I'm sure…"

"It's David." He smiled. "We have all day. Couple of days."

What about his life? When did he begin his search for spirit?

"When I was 14 I was a paperboy in rural Wisconsin with a 17 mile route. One night I was caught in a 20 below zero blizzard. Falling off my bicycle, I dug a hole in the ice crust and huddled in a snow cave to try to keep warm. My clothes were frozen stiff, I was weeping in terror. Soon, the shivering stopped, and there was a delicious warmth, and then a state of peace beyond all description. This was accompanied by a suffusion of light and a presence of infinite love which had no beginning and no end and which was undifferentiated from my own essence. My mind grew silent. All thought stopped. An infinite Presence was all that was or could be. The concept of death seemed absurd to me.

"Uncounted time later, my father pulled me out of the snowbank. I felt most reluctant to return to the body and all that it entailed, but I loved my father dearly, and because of his anguish I chose that. Later, I didn't discuss my experience with anyone. There was no context available with which to comprehend it. After it, the accepted reality of the world began to seem only provisional. Traditional religious experience lost significance, and, paradoxically, I became an agnostic. Compared to the light of divinity which I had felt bathing all existence, the God of traditional religion shone dully indeed. I had lost religion but discovered spirituality."

What about in the war, David? You were in the Navy?

"Yes. I'd been assigned to hazardous duty on a minesweeper." (In amusement, he showed me pictures of himself as a very young sailor, arm around his buddies. We swapped a few tales about the Pacific. He'd only come out toward the end of the war, but we might have crossed paths when I was flying out of Okinawa.) "Often, I brushed close to death, but unlike the other crew members, I had no fear of it. It was as if death had lost its authenticity. After the war, fascinated by the complexities of the mind and wanting to study psychiatry, I worked my way through medical school. My training psychoanalyst, a professor at Columbia University, was also an agnostic. We both took a dim view of religion. The analysis went well, as did my career, and I became quite successful.

"I did not, however, settle quietly into professional life. I fell ill with a progressive and fatal illness which did not respond to any treatments available. By the age of 38, I was in extremis and knew I was about to die. I didn't care about the body, but my spirit was in a state of extreme anguish and despair. As the final moment approached, the thought flashed through my mind, "What if there is a God?" So I called out in prayer, 'If there is a God, I ask him to help me now.' I surrendered to whatever God

179

there might be, and went unconscious, and when I awoke, a transformation of such enormity had taken place that I was struck dumb with awe.

"The person I had been no longer existed. There was no personal self or ego, only an Infinite Presence of such unlimited power that it was all that was. The Presence had replaced what had been 'me,' and my body and its actions were controlled solely by the Infinite Will of the Presence. The world was illuminated by the clarity of an Infinite Oneness which expressed itself as all things revealed in their infinite beauty and perfection."

What did the experience feel like?

"Stillness. For nine months it persisted. I had no will of my own. My physical entity went about its business under the direction of the infinitely powerful, but exquisitely gentle, will of the Presence. In that state, there was no need to think about anything. All truth was self-evident. There was nothing to seek. All was perfect. Fame, success, money were meaningless. However, I discovered that I could perceive the reality that underlay personalities. I saw how the origin of emotional sickness lay in people's belief that they were their personalities. And so, of its own, my practice resumed and eventually became huge."

This was in New York?

"Yes, at Columbia. People came from all over the United States and sometimes as far away as Germany and Egypt. I had fifty therapists and other employees, two thousand outpatients, a suite of 25 offices, research and electro-encephalic laboratories, and treated a thousand new patients a year. I was invited to appear on radio and network television: McNeil/Lehrer, Today, Barbara Walters. I reported the work I was doing in a traditional format in the book Orthomolecular Psychiatry, co-authored with Linus Pauling. This work, ten years ahead of its time, created something of a stir."

You write that during those years, you were able to perform quite amazing healings. Had you found some new sort of power?

"All mankind is motivated by inner love, but has simply become unaware. Most lives are lived by sleepers unawakened to the awareness of who they really are. All those around me looked as through they were asleep, but incredibly beautiful. I was in love with everyone."

Did this affect your own healing?

"Absolutely. Many chronic maladies I had suffered for years disappeared. I saw that all pain and suffering arises solely from the ego and not from God. This was a truth which I silently communicated to the minds of my patients. Once, when I intuited a mental block in a particular catatonic who had not spoken in many years, and said to him, through my mind, "You're blaming God for what your ego has done to you," he jumped off the floor and began to speak, much to the surprise of the nurse who witnessed the incident."

How long did you practice this way?

"Quite a few years. But the work had become increasingly taxing. Patients were backed up waiting for beds, even though the hospital had put on another wing to accommodate my overload. The tide of human suffering was like bailing out the sea. I felt that there must be some way to address the causes of the common malaise, the endless stream of spiritual distress and human suffering. It was about then that I came onto kinesiology, and it seemed to provide an answer."

You write that the mind thinks with the body?

"Unquestionably. I saw kinesiology as the wormhole between the two universes, physical and spirit. People are affected by what thoughts they hold in their minds. But exceptional, subjective experiences of truth are the province of the mystic."

In what way?

"The mystic affects all mankind by sending forth the energy of his level into the collective consciousness. This is the function of the attractor fields where the electrical energy is stored. Unfortunately, the process is not understandable to the majority of mankind, and therefore is of limited meaning except to other spiritual seekers. When I realized this, I sought now to get down on the mundane level, to be ordinary because just being ordinary in itself is an expression of divinity. The truth of one's real self can be discovered through the pathway of everyday life. To live

181

with care and kindness is all that's necessary."

You write that you'd had a wonderful life in New York...

"All the trappings anyone would want. The apartment on Park Avenue, the eighty acre estate on Long Island. I was in love with French chateaus. I went to France, studied the architecture and built my own castle. Hard to give up, the most difficult thing in my life."

Then why did you do it?

"After a long circular journey to the spirit, I returned to the most important work, which is to bring the Presence that has moved my life perhaps a little closer to the grasp of as many of my fellow beings as I can."

That's what brought you to Rattlebone Ranch?

"The main obstacle to human development is the lack of knowledge about the nature of consciousness itself. Medicine has forgotten that it is an art, with science merely a tool of that art. Only a few have gone beyond the parameters of their fields to investigate the nature of consciousness itself and its relationship between the universe and science.That's what I'm doing here, trying to marry the two. "

Do you have any particular goal in mind?

"All human endeavor has the common goal of understanding or influencing human experience. The frenetic search is the expectation of finding an ultimate 'answer' that will allow us to solve the problems of human existence. We are virtually drowning in data but don't have the tools to interpret it. We mis-identify our own intellectual artifacts as reality. Moral systems reduce the enormous complexity of human behavior into right or wrong. Psychoanalysis has compounded this muddle."

So what IS the answer?

"Humans lift themselves by their bootstraps by effortlessly rising to a higher state of consciousness. Force cannot accomplish this. Power constantly does. Throughout history society has tried to treat social problems by legislative action, warfare, market manipulation, laws and prohibitions. These are all manifestations of force. But power is effortless. It goes unseen and unsuspected, unlike force which is felt through the senses. Power can only be recognized through inner awareness.

We are immobilized in our present condition by our alignment with enormously powerful attractor energy patterns. Moment by moment we are suspended in this state, restrained by the energies of force, impelled by the energies of power. We are like corks in the sea of consciousness, floating about in endless conundrums, asking the same questions. Only through leaps in consciousness do we advance."

Can anyone make such a leap?

"Possible---perhaps not likely. Few people follow the steps because they are so simple."

You mean we don't understand them?

"Spiritual joy occurs on a quiet level of inexplicable ecstacy. Because the experience of time stops, there is no apprehension or regret, nor pain, nor anticipation. The source of joy is unending and ever present. With no beginning or ending, there is no loss or grief or desire. Nothing needs to be done. Everything is already perfect and complete.

Is there any way you can teach such a state of awareness?'

I can only share my own experience:

"First, my desire to reach that state was intense.

"Then began the discipline to act with constant and universal forgiveness and gentleness, without exception. One has to be compassionate toward everything, including one's own self and thoughts.

"Next came a willingness to hold desires in abeyance and surrender personal will at every moment. As each thought, feeling, desire or deed was surrendered to God, the mind became increasingly silent. At first, I turned over whole stories and paragraphs, then ideas and concepts. As one lets go of wanting to own these thoughts, they no longer reach such elaboration, and begin to fragment while only half formed.

"Finally, I could turn over the energy behind the thought itself, before it even became thought.

"The task of constant, unrelenting fixity of focus, allowing not even a moment of distraction continued while doing ordinary activities. As time went on, it became habitual, like a rocket leaving earth, at first requiring tremendous power but then less and less as it moves through space under its own momentum."

And once you get there, if you do, could you describe what you found?

"As the ego died, it was replaced by the Self as Everythingness, the All in which everything is known and obvious in its perfect expression of its own essence. With non-locality came the awareness that one is all that ever was or can be. One is total and complete, beyond all identities, beyond gender, beyond even humanness itself. One need never again fear suffering and death.

"The body appears as an "it" rather than a "me," another object like the furniture in the room.There is no way to explain this state of unawareness to the unaware. It is best to go on about one's business and let Providence handle the social adjustment. But one may become a magnet to the spiritual seekers and the very ill, and a source of joy to them. There is a desire to share this state with others, and use it for the benefit of all….

Are you saying that you've now surrendered the ego?

"Everything. In this final apocalypse of the self, you've not only dissolved the sole remaining duality---that of existence and non-existence---but you've dissolved your identity itself into universal divinity, and no individual consciousness is left to choose. The last step, then, is taken by God alone…"

At that point, though Teddy was still bright-eyed and yearning for more, I was sprawled on the sofa, my brain feeling as if I'd just run through a heavy artillery barrage. David Hawkins was truly an incredible teacher. In his video tapes, he'll talk without notes for twenty minutes or longer in a single camera take, no cuts to catch his breath, never straying from his train of thought, and tossing in throwaway lines that are so loaded with meaning they blow your mind. I've elided his words here, simply because you just can't get him the first time around.

Like David, we'd lost track of time and hunger. The lunches went uneaten but the sun kept cooking the trailer, albeit at mercifully decreasing angles. Teddy was doggedly taking notes, but by then, I was going to wait for the video. I was so intellectually strung out, all I could catch were a few of David's memorable bullets.

---"No one has any idea what Jesus Christ said about

reincarnation. In fact, we really don't know what he said about anything. Whatever he taught has been edited.

---"If you calibrate the energy of Christianity in the first century, it was about 925. Then in the year 485, around the time of the council of Nicea, it dropped precipitously, the worst spiritual catastrophe in history. Using kinesiology, you could go into the council of Nicea, see who was there, what was decided, the denigration of the body, etc., and determine the reasons for this dramatic loss of truth."

---"I always felt Jesus was very practical, since the best the average person could hope for is one of the higher heavens. What Jesus taught is to develop good karma, avoid negative karma and you will land in one of the higher heavens. The heavenly hosts are full of enlightened teachers and in their presence you can go into very high states of awareness."

---"That which is the I which gives a sense of reality is not the individual I but is actually the existence of God within oneself. Without the presence of God there would be no life. That's what's comical about the athiest because the God within is what allows one to say, 'I don't believe in God,' which is a left brain process."

---"God and I are both honored by capitalization. If the I were only the ego it would be small i. But everywhere in the world I is capitalized just as God is capitalized "

---"Simple kindness to oneself and all that lives is the most powerful transformational force of all. But to reach maximum power it must be practiced with no exceptions nor with the expectation of some selfish reward."

For the rest of the afternoon and well into the next day, our questioning led David to address the problems of modern society, literally the sickness of the American soul. "The great source of negativity today," he said, "is through the media, through Rap music, the glamorization of the trivial, the tremendous power that programming and advertising have over people, the destruction of youth through consumerism and violence. Dark forces through the media are infecting large segments of our youth. We have a large percentage of youth growing up today who have already been destroyed and

185

entrained into powerful negative energy fields. The glamour figures who are worshipped today are dominated by negative energy fields. There are nights on TV where every channel is devoted to murder or some sort of depravity."

Why so much negativity? "Because most people are living in the lower levels of fear and guilt. This is what fascinates them. Almost everyone in America is suffering from Post Traumatic Stress Disorder.

"Corporations own the media. There is a deliberate dumbing down. The law of society now is the bottom line. It is a culture of ego-centricity and satiation of material wants and artificial pleasures brought about by the media."

Where is this going to lead us?

"We are spiraling down in certain segments of society. Other segments are going up. People are not interested in spiritually evolving until their physical needs are taken care of. You have entire sub-continents who live on the edge of starvation. As you fulfill their material desires, they begin to look for something better.

"The advertising media is caught in the level of desire. The process here is entrapment. Wantingness is an on-going state. Like any addiction, there is no satiation point. Wantingness is the opposite of that which is real, which is in the exact moment now. All the lower levels take you out of the now. Fear takes you into the past, desire into the future, anger into the past. We have a perpetually unfulfilled culture.

"The source of all joy is in the radical instant of the *now*." At this point, David got up and began acting out comically what he was trying to explain. "A man is in prison and going to be executed. He is sitting in the cell waiting for the jailor to take him to the guillotine. I ask him, 'Do you have a problem now?' He begins to mumble that he didn't sleep well last night. 'That's past. I want now. Do you have a problem NOW?'

"'Well, no. But my stomach was off this morning, worrying about the knife.'

"'That's future! Do you have a problem NOW?"

"'No.'"

Crouching over, David walks down the corridor with the

doomed man. At each step, "'Do you have a problem now?'"

"'No.'"

Second step, third step, all No's, the man reaches the guillotine and lays his head on the block. The blade rises above his head. "'Do you have a problem now?'"

"'No.'"

"If you are living in the exact moment you are not having a problem. Whack! His head is severed. At the instant of death, his spirit arises and he witnesses his head roll away. No one experiences his own death. It is not possible. At the moment of death, one goes out of body and witnesses what is happening in the phenomenal world but it is not possible to experience your own actual death."

By this time, late the second afternoon in the hot trailer, the death I was experiencing was of my own certitudes. It was the end of "I know." The surrender to spirit was the last letting go, the humbling and the agony of realizing how little I knew.

In the lengthening shadows, Teddy tried to sum up her feelings. Her lip began to tremble. She described her spiritual searching she'd done all her life, the prayers, the retreats. "I want so much to love God and be good," she began to say, but never finished. She covered her face in her hands and wept.

In a wisp of his organic tobacco, David put down his moldy old pipe, moved his chair next to Teddy's. Gently, he took her wrists in his hands. ""All your prayers, all your retreats," he said quietly, "that's fine, if you enjoy them. But they're quite irrelevant. They're not really you. You already have your way."

Her head lifted, her cheeks wet.

"Your way," he said, "is devotion."

In that instant, I saw her entire life rush past, this girl I'd loved for so long. I choked up, too. We sat in silence. With the brilliance of a laser beam, he had illuminated her meaning.

19.

Not long after we'd visited David Hawkins in Arizona, he sent Teddy the draft of a short piece he'd written for a scientific magazine. It moved us so much that I incorporated his meditative practice into my own attempts with my K-mart candle.

The Realization of the Presence of God

Spiritual information is so vast and students so diverse in their respective levels of development, many seekers are now in an overwhelm.

What to do with it all?

Write affirmations, recite mantras, be lightworkers, get readings, channelings, do colors, rays, vibrations, numbers, crystals, amulets, gatherings, workshops, seminars. Chase gurus, go to Katmandu, India, Stonehenge, take more courses, listen to more tapes, go on strange diets, do exercises, assume poses, breathe in all kinds of bizarre manners. Get re-born, change names, wear funny clothes, give up shoes for sandals, give up sex, have more sex in strained styles. Live in dirty, cramped quarters, on rice only, get beriberi, get crazy haircuts, wear orange knit hats, mortify the flesh, starve, flagellate. Play American Indian, play East Indian, visit Shamans, chant in foreign languages, beat drums, wear feathers, worship nature, get initiated, wear all white, all yellow, all saffron. Shave your head, fiind a cult, disown your family, leave your friends, desert your spouse, swear allegiance to an egomaniac, commit group suicide.

Now what?

Real spiritual advancement requires the sometimes painful move from naivete to wisdom, the letting go of the seductive trappings that entrap. When you really understand Zen, you let go of Zen-ness, gongs, rice bowls and trying to speak Japanese.

It's time to get real.

All spiritual truth is contained in every spiritual concept. It is only necessary to totally understand one single concept to understand them all, and arrive at the realization of the Real. Choose one concept or spiritual tool and pursue it relentlessly to its ultimate end: forgiveness of kindness carried to the absolute, the 3rd step from a 12 step program, whatever. Then apply it to every single thought, feeling, action, behavior without exception.

It only takes a single scalpel to dissect the entire human body and it only takes a single spiritual scalpel to dissect oneself free of the ego. In the beginning it requires effort to overcome innate resistance, but when willingness is perfected through progressive surrender, the tool takes on a life of its own---there is no longer a "me" to do it.

One eventually realizes the tool is being guided by something other than the personal self. One does not "find" the truth, so it is futile to "seek" it. Divinity reveals itself effortlessly. It is a matter of preparing for it through the agony of dying to our small self, to our personal agenda.

It is the heart that is at one with God, not the mind. The intellect is the block. Love heals the suffering of the world. To discover one's own heart is to discover God.

What is the simplest meditative practice?

I think you should just sit with your arms slightly raised and hands held out, not to receive as in the Eastern tradition, but on the contrary, to radiate out that which you would give to the world. As you do this, you awaken to what the world is crying for and automatically you radiate that and you suddenly realize who you are. Sitting quietly with hands held out as if to bless the world, you become a channel of God and radiate out unconditional love. You give all that you are infinitely capable of giving. You are an antenna of radiance, a radical laser beam.

You keep doing that, and that which humanity needs will reveal itself to you, and that which humanity intrinsically is will reveal itself to you and eventually that which is the Real Self will shine forth in an Absolute Harmonious Perfection.

The mind is stilled. There is no "here" or "there," no subject or object, no "me" or "you." Nothing is causing anything. Everything already is as is. There is no discontinuity. Everything is one.

The illusion is that one struggles with spiritual growth by one's own effort, but in fact we are pulled into greater awareness by the Will of God expressed as the Holy Spirit and all that is necessary is to allow it to happen by surrendering completely.

For truly, only God is God.

20.

When Teddy and I first moved to our ranch on the Green River of Wyoming, an old cowboy warned us: "If you don't like the weather up here in these mountains, wait a minute. She'll change on you in the wink of an eyelash. You start out riding, your horse will be pawing ice. Before you know it, you're sweltering, stripping off your heavies and rolling up your shirtsleeves. Or she'll go the other way. Dry as a bone when you leave the barn, dust devils whirling up. Whooee! Minute later, here's this big black booger of a cloud, lightning cracking into the sage, hail balls size of a half dollar hammering you. So when you leave the barn, pack all the gear you got. Even then, it may not be enough, for the changeyness of it."

But now, thirty-six years later, Teddy and I were riding out into an August morning that couldn't possibly have any changeyness in it. The sun was an egg yolk sliding across a blue bowl of sky. The granite turrets of the Wind River mountains glittered golden, and the forests of lodgepole on their slopes were like dark sentries guarding their treasure. The air was so sweet with pine and sage that we wanted to bottle it and smell it forever.

We were twenty miles north of our ranch, up by the rock fist of Squaretop Mountain. It's a postcard, so spectacular that Salem cigarettes once used it as the centerpiece of their TV commercial. The ad men love this country. They found their first Marlboro man here, Darryl Winfield, an old friend with whom we've horse-traded and cowboyed. For years now, his successor Marlboro clones have been galloping across these same sagebrush valleys, connoting ruggedness, freedom, macho---and while you're at it, puff yourself away like Duke Wayne.

They've all trooped off into the darkness, Duke, leaving it colored red and riding into the sunset of his feisty hunting ground in the sky. The happy little Monroe family found Pa's valley all right, only to be driven from it by a leaden hail of lousy network ratings. Winners, losers, Barry Goldwater gone to his defeat, LBJ to his short-lived victory before Vietnam did him in. Ronnie Reagan had found the Russians human after all, and plunged so tragically into Alzheimers that he couldn't remember his Evil Empire and the steps he'd finally taken to dismantle it.

In the end, it comes down to <u>Choice</u>, the film unseen, the question unanswered. Which kind of America do we want? What do we have to do to make it happen?

The choice is with you and me. It's the letting go to spirit, and the humility to admit that all for all of our huffing and puffing all the years, Humpty Dumpty will be in parts and pieces until we can heal him, each of us, in our American soul.

But this morning on the Green, the sound and fury of the madding crowd seemed far too distant to hear. I followed Teddy down the slippery river bank. Our horses sniffed the water, balked and then at a touch of our heels, plunged in. We'd slog across and God willing locate two hundred and fifty black heifers scattered somewhere on the other side. If we lucked into them, we'd cut out the foot rots, cancer eyes or otherwise unfortunates that needed doctoring. Count numbers, wondering all the while where the missing ones could possibly have gone, and if we could ever get them home.

Above us, the granite turret of Squaretop lay reflected in the still azure mirror of Green River Lake. The great river begins here and flows south, joining the Colorado and finally spilling thousands of miles below into the hot, coppery Gulf of California.

It only seemed a moment ago when Teddy and I had been walking the sands of a long Mexican beach, very near where our river mingled with the salt of the Pacific. At that time, we'd had a ranch in the Arizona desert. It was close enough to the Baja peninsula and the Gulf that we'd drive down often. I'd fish, she'd study her Spanish or spiritual works, and in a day or two, the worries of praying for rain on a desert ranch were lapped away by the Pacific waves.

The horse I was riding today on the Green had been born on the Arizona ranch. I'd named him Baboquivari for the sacred peak of the Papago Indians that rose up in the mountains behind our adobe house. But the name was too much of a mouthful, so for twenty years he's been just plain Bobby. Often now, I stroke his neck and tell him, "Old Bob, you're the last best horse I'll ever have." I think he knows what I mean.

I'd bred him to race. His father held the mile and a sixteenth record at Santa Anita. But when Bobby was only a new-born wobbly colt, a mountain lion stalked him. Bobby plunged into the side of our mesquite wood corral and blinded himself in one eye. Noble as he was, he tried to race, but rival jockeys would slam into his blind side, and finally I took him home to breed us some foals and carry me around. From then on, we became a pair of ex-competitors, he clacking me nobly and up the rocky canyons of Arizona, and when we'd left them behind, he'd lugged me for twenty years out through the oaks and chamiso jungles of our California ranch.

And now, this morning on the Green, the California ranch was gone, too. We'd sold out. In a U-Haul, a trailer and two old Ford station wagons, we'd hauled up horses, dogs, cat, all the baggage of our lives, arriving finally at the only land we had left. The place where our western adventure had begun, Wyoming, Bobby and me, going around the track together one last time.

Though the Green was reasonably shallow where we were now crossing, Bobby's feet were slipping on the rocky bottom. Occasionally he'd stumble into a deep hole, snort in distaste and hunch up. I whispered him: "You cranky old bastard, don't you go bucking like a colt." Then he picked up his head and glanced at his younger brother, Little Boy, whom Teddy was riding just ahead of us. Little Boy's registered name is Seedskadee, meaning in Shoshone the sage grouse and/or the Green River which is their habitat. One of our granddaughters couldn't cope with it and just shortened him to Little Boy. Turning in her saddle, Teddy glanced back at me. "Can't you get him across?"

"Of course I can. You just worry about you." By then, Bobby was in a hole, up to his shoulders in water. I hadn't pulled out of the stirrups quick enough and my boots got a soak. When we reached the other side, Bobby shook himself angrily. Then, in his old habit, he twisted his neck around and bit the toe of my boot. It was always his signal. Get done what we have to do, damn you, and then let me get the hell home!

The land where we were searching for the heifers is a grazing allotment on the National Forest, a wilderness of 17,000 acres, bisected by the Green River and Roaring Fork creek. That morning, it felt to me like 170,000 acres, a vastness of sagebrush ridges rising into forests of aspen and higher, dark stands of lodgepole. Teddy and I have cowboyed together for nearly 40 years. Sometimes the vistas are so spectacular---the tawny sweep of the Arizona desert, the oaken valleys and golden hills of California, or the seas of sagebrush in Wyoming---in those moments, we rein in our horses and just stare at it in wonder. Often, we'll lean across our saddles and hug each other in thanks. We don't deserve the splendor that's here.

But today, we had to split up, searching for 250 black needles in an immense haystack. Teddy dropped over the first ridge and into the willows of Roaring Fork Valley. For all these years, Little Boy has taken good care of her, and I blessed him for that. Like his eminent father, he'd also raced at Santa Anita, and was so tightly wound that if Teddy's heels happened to brush his flank, he'd catapult out as if from the starting gate. But now, he was just patiently dogging along. From above, I watched her until she was a tiny shadow, hunting diligently for black hides in the willows.

I turned Bobby and climbed a thousand feet higher into the cliffs of dark timber where the elk lived and lately, grizzly bears, expanding their range. They were killing cattle in the area. I hoped I wouldn't find gnawed carcasses of ours. As Bobby picked his way through the blowdowns of lodgepole, he'd creak up his legs painfully and I could almost hear him sigh, longing for his short, pampered days on the racetrack. Soon the timber closed around us and became as sepulchral as an abandoned church. It was empty, no game, not even birds. The only sound was Bobby's hooves, tocking against fallen logs.

I needed the silence of it right then. The sale of the California ranch had been an agonizing decision for Teddy and me. From our first days of courting, we'd always dreamed of living out on the land and telling its stories. We'd bonded on it for forty years, rooted in, rooted out, shed the tears, lived with the fears of bad cattle markets and unknown challenges that sprung from owning so much land. Perhaps that was our final reason for selling. We'd done it, built it, but now our beloved golden hills were just too much for the autumn of our lives. In our 20 square miles of paradise, there were hidden canyons I'd never live long enough to explore. There were brushy mountain peaks that I once had scrambled up after a covey of quail, but now my legs were telling me: let 'em go, let 'em live.

For all the joys of the ranch we'd shared, we seemed to be taking up too much space.

Let go, our spirit was whispering. Happiness is not a place. It's not owning land because you never really do own it. You just borrow it for a while from the All. It's not owning cows or beloved horses or bird dogs. Own-own-own, our culture tells us. But happiness only owns itself. It's not the three states where we'd ranched, it's the state of our spirits.

For six years, we'd been trying to sell the ranch, and now that we had, a knife seemed to be twisting in our hearts. What we'd cut out of ourselves was an image that we'd once seemed to demand. It was the specialness of owning a kingdom, of laying up a splendid treasure of earth. But did we really need all that anymore? Wasn't it finally time to simplify, cut down, and love what we still have? Take the other turn in the road, let the spirit guide, and pray for the courage to make another leap out into the unknown.

Our three sons were long raised and gone, our six grandchildren growing up fast. We missed them all, we loved them, but the bottom line was: we were coming home alone now, just the two of us, starting all over again the way we'd begun.

Riding on for the next several hours, I covered more timber and high country meadows than I hoped to see. I never stumbled onto a single heifer. Where the devil could they be hiding? But the unknowing went with the territory. For the next month of roundup, we'd be finding and losing and finding again, until one day we'd whoop and holler them into a bunch and trail them home. God willing.

In the splendid silence of the search, I thought of all the sure things I'd clung to for so long, the delusions that my intellectual artifacts were reality, and that because of them I KNEW THE WAY. I could find the beasts, line them out on the trail and cash in at the end. In my writing and speaking, I could even pretend to answer the earnest people who always seemed to be asking: What can any of us DO about the state of our nation? Give us prescriptions, road signs, quit running down that dead end and try this one.

We're all longing for somebody, even a nobody like me, to determine our future. But determine, I'd come to realize, means to terminate. Put the future in a neat box, wrap a fundamentalist ribbon around it and say, That's that!

But, like the wandering heifers, spirit won't let itself be corralled. The life force refuses to be terminated. That's the mystery of it, and the harrowing fear for those who demand certainty.

Higher up the great valley of the Green River, I could see naked slabs of granite, above timberline. Fringing them were the last tiny, scraggly trees. Instinctively, those trees must have known that they were out of their element, and thus had made themselves smaller to cope with high altitudes.

They were programmed to survive.

You and I are far more sensitive than a tree.

The sensitivity of your spirit and the spirits of enough people will eventually adjust us to the element we find ourselves in. They will self-correct our systems and conform them to the needs of our survival.

Money can't buy spirit.

Force can't take away its power.

Like the trees, spirit has programmed you and me to seek the survival that has been coded into us by the life force.

Corporate control, the goods myth and the demon of Enemies Out There are subject to these same truths. They crush souls, they are not supportive of life, which is why, eventually, they, like all the other great enslavements of humankind, have been ended and will continue to be ended by rising consciousness.

It's already beginning to happen. Experts in many fields are writing books or speaking out on the specific changes needed to support life. The solutions exist. They're an electrical energy in the attractor field of human emotions. They're already in place in the minds of gifted men and women, and in the sensitive intuition of ordinary citizens.

Instinctively, you know that most of the structures of our society were created by low energy, bottom of the box emotions. By force, used against you. Force systems created your monsters and you've had to resort to force to fight against them. Why is it that you so often feel un-represented, alienated, powerless? How do you respond? Isn't it in Shame: despising, miserable, humiliation? If you rise just one step, your response is Guilt, vindictive, suffering, blame, self-hate. Still higher, you go into Apathy: condemning, hopeless, despair, dropping out. Then upward, into Grief: regret, loss, despondency. At this point, Fear seizes you: punitive, frightening, anxiety, panic. If you happen to be slightly higher on the dreary totem pole, Desire grips you: frustrated, disappointing, addiction, craving, enslavement. Once you're here, fully recognizing your plight, you go into Anger: competitive, antagonistic, hate, grievance, aggression. And last, up into Pride: demanding, denial, scorn, arrogance, self-inflation.

If you respond to the force systems and their myths in such a way, how do you ever get free of the monsters? How do you take your power back into yourself?

You tap into the synchronicity of your spirit. Let go and allow it to happen. Let God.

Humanity doesn't wave a wand and make its problems go away. It's a process. A few people at a time begin making their leaps to the positive energies of courage and the higher emotions. Discovery occurs here. They begin to see the lie of many of our systems. They reconceptualize antiquated political parties, the purchase of power by a few to the exclusion of the many. Their risen consciousness shows them the lie of giving unrestricted influence to corporations, treating them as fictitious entities rather than as responsible citizens. They begin to see the lie of a liar's tax code, a fraudulent Drug War, and a rapacious global empire-making where the few reap the profits and the many do the paying and the dying. In the critical mass of these exposures, the seedbed of our new world is slowly beginning to sprout.

Mankind has always lived primarily in the low, negative emotions. But now, because of technology---not in spite of it---more people than ever before have access to truth and to lie. It is this tantalizing dichotomy---which road shall we choose?---that puts us on the brink of a spiritual explosion unparalleled in history.

When our consciousness---yours, mine and millions of others---lifts us high enough in our emotions, the BE of our spirit power is going to fuse with the DO of our force, and in the higher voltage joining of these positive electricities, we are slowly going to melt into One, the All. In our unity in diversity, we are going to see how to solve what we never could before.

Letting go of our old positions, our rigid concepts of right or wrong, lifting to Reason and finally to Compassion, the synchronicity of consciousness---being in the right place with the right message at the right time---will cause the old structures to change.

The change is in ourselves.

Living as much as possible in your exact now, you will begin to see what you must BE and DO to help lift your society out of its darkness. You become a missionary of the spirit, slowly knowing what you didn't know you knew, and at last, how to put it into action.

Reach that point, and you will have given up the war in yourself by surrendering to your spirit.

You may dread it, weep over it, but in the end, when you have risen high enough in your healing emotions, spirit will make the choice for you.

It will guide you to truth, and to your survival.

But that morning on the Green River, the future was only a fleeting dream. In the reality of the present, I was too saddle-sore and weary of searching for heifers that weren't there, and now, apparently, neither was Teddy. In the past we'd had rides where she'd get tangled up in old barbed wire, or a tree branch would knock her out of her saddle. More likely, she'd become so engrossed by the scenery or picking wildflowers that she'd lose her way. Once in the California Sierras, she'd wandered for hours from twilight into night above timberline and finally ran smack into a big black object, looming above her. She froze, speechless in terror. When it didn't move, she roared: "Are you a bear?"

No, just a swatch of lichen on a big white rock. By then, far below, I was firing my .22 revolver at regular intervals, booming out a desperate radar signal to my lost heroine. She finally heard and came tumbling down the mountain where I took a scared and thoroughly wiped out lady into my arms.

But today, muttering that she was lost again, I came over the last ridge above the Green and there she was. Of all things, she'd found another rock, this time a table-like slab of granite, rumbled down eons before by some retreating ice age. It was all by itself in the tall, swaying grass.

She was stretched out on it sound asleep, and looked to me as young and lovely as she had on the sand at Paradise Island, or even falling down the stairs into my lap fifty-two years ago. I dismounted and took my own doze beside her. Time didn't matter. We had noplace to hurry off to. When she awakened, she stared wistfully out across the valley. "Just think," she murmured, "of all the people who can never see this. I feel like we're seeing it for them, aren't we?"

I kissed her and held her. Then I cinched up the horses and when Bobby glared at me, I said, "Come on, old man. It's time."

Together we rode back again, down by the riverside.
Home again from paradise,
Wondering why, wondering how,
And knowing too well that if we've found anything at all,
It's only in this moment now.

www.ingramcontent.com/pod-product-compliance
Lightning Source LLC
Chambersburg PA
CBHW030435290526
45786CB00001B/301